Tribute to Henry A. "Hank" Ross

THIS WORKBOOK SERIES is dedicated to the legacy of Henry A. "Hank" Rosso, noted by many experts as one of the leading figures in the development of organized philanthropic fund raising in the twentieth century. This series of workbooks, ranging from *Developing Your Case for Support* to *Building Your Endowment,* was the last project he undertook before his health failed him. The Indiana University Center on Philanthropy, of which he was a founder, is honored to have been asked to complete this project on Hank's behalf. My colleagues and I dedicate this series to his memory.

I am grateful to my colleague Tim Seiler for agreeing to serve as editor. Tim is director of The Fund Raising School, the national and international training program that Hank started in 1974. It is appropriate that this workbook series be tied directly to concepts and materials taught by The Fund Raising School.

By carefully studying the practitioners and scholars in fund raising who came before him, Hank was able to codify and teach principles and techniques for effective philanthropic fund raising. Scores of practitioners who applied his principles have been successful in diversifying their philanthropic fund raising and donor bases in sustaining their worthy causes. Hank was constantly concerned that those who might most need the information of The Fund Raising School might be least able to access it. He developed special courses for small organizations and edited *Achieving Excellence in Fund Raising* to get information into the hands of practitioners. This workbook series was for Hank another attempt to put the tools of effective philanthropic fund raising into the hands of practitioners who could not get to The Fund Raising School courses.

We hope you find this material useful to you in your work. One of Hank's favorite sayings was, "You can raise a lot more money with organized fund raising than you can with disorganized fund raising." We hope it helps you organize and find success in your fund raising activities. As you carry out your work, remember Hank's definition: "Fund raising is the gentle art of teaching the joy of giving."

Eugene R. Tempel
Executive Director
Indiana University Center on Philanthropy

EXCELLENCE IN FUND RAISING WORKBOOK SERIES TITLES AVAILABLE NOW:

THE JOSSEY–BASS NONPROFIT AND PUBLIC MANAGEMENT SERIES ALSO INCLUDES:

The Excellence in Fund Raising Workbook Series

EXCELLENCE IN
FUND RAISING

WORKBOOK SERIES

THE FUND RAISING WORKBOOK SERIES began with Hank Rosso and his vision of a set of separate yet interrelated workbooks designed to offer practical, high-quality models for successful fund raising. Each workbook focuses on a single topic and provides narrative material explaining the topic, worksheets, sample materials, and other practical advice. Designed and written for fund raising professionals, nonprofit leaders, and volunteers, the workbooks provide models and strategies for carrying out successful fund raising programs. The texts are based on the accumulated experience and wisdom of veteran fund raising professionals as validated by research, theory, and practice. Each workbook stands alone yet is part of a bigger whole. The workbooks are similar in format and design and use as their primary textual content the curriculum of The Fund Raising School as originally developed and written by Hank Rosso, Joe Mixer, and Lyle Cook. Hank selected or suggested authors for the series and intended to be coeditor of the series. The authors stay true to Hank's philosophy of fund raising, and the series is developed as a form of stewardship to Hank's ideals of ethical fund raising. All authors address how their contributions to the series act in tandem with the other steps in Hank's revolutionary Fund Raising Cycle, as illustrated here. It is the intent of the editor and of the publisher that this will be the premier hands-on workbook series for fund raisers and their volunteers.

Dedicated to
the advancement
of ethical
fund raising

**The
Fund Raising
School**

Timothy L. Seiler

General Series Editor

Director, The Fund Raising School

Indiana University Center on Philanthropy

The Fund Raising Cycle

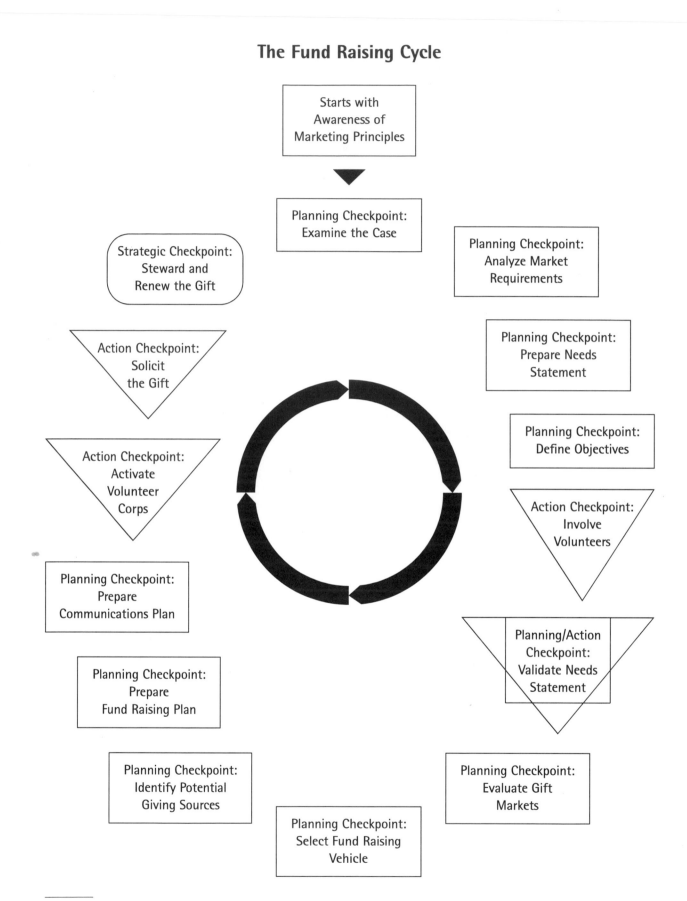

Starts with
Awareness of
Marketing Principles

Planning Checkpoint:
Examine the Case

Planning Checkpoint:
Analyze Market
Requirements

Strategic Checkpoint:
Steward and
Renew the Gift

Planning Checkpoint:
Prepare Needs
Statement

Action Checkpoint:
Solicit
the Gift

Planning Checkpoint:
Define Objectives

Action Checkpoint:
Activate
Volunteer
Corps

Action Checkpoint:
Involve
Volunteers

Planning Checkpoint:
Prepare
Communications Plan

Planning/Action
Checkpoint:
Validate Needs
Statement

Planning Checkpoint:
Prepare
Fund Raising Plan

Planning Checkpoint:
Identify Potential
Giving Sources

Planning Checkpoint:
Evaluate Gift
Markets

Planning Checkpoint:
Select Fund Raising
Vehicle

Source: Henry A. Rosso and Associates, *Achieving Excellence in Fund Raising,* p. 10. Copyright © 1991 Jossey-Bass Inc., Publishers. Reprinted by permission of John Wiley & Sons, Inc.

BUILDING YOUR ENDOWMENT

EXCELLENCE IN
FUND RAISING

WORKBOOK SERIES

Series Editor
Timothy L. Seiler

BUILDING YOUR ENDOWMENT

EDWARD C. SCHUMACHER

JOSSEY-BASS
A Wiley Imprint
www.josseybass.com

Published by Jossey-Bass
A Wiley Imprint
989 Market Street, San Francisco, CA 94103-1741   www.josseybass.com

Jossey-Bass books and products are available through most bookstores. To contact Jossey-Bass directly call our Customer Care Department within the U.S. at 800-956-7739, outside the U.S. at 317-572-3986 or fax 317-572-4002.

Jossey-Bass also publishes its books in a variety of electronic formats. Some content that appears in print may not be available in electronic books.

Library of Congress Cataloging-in-Publication Data

Schumacher, Edward C.
     Building your endowment/Edward C. Schumacher.
         p. cm.—(The Jossey-Bass nonprofit and public management
series)
     ISBN 0-7879-6010-1 (alk. paper)
     1. Nonprofit organizations—Endowments. 2. Fund raising. I. Title.
II. Series.
   HG4027.65.S38 2002
   658.15'224—dc21

                                        2002155389

Printed in the United States of America

The Jossey-Bass
Nonprofit and Public Management Series

Contents

Exhibits and Worksheets

Chapter 5

Preface

YEAR IN AND YEAR OUT, nonprofit organizations are asked to serve more people, provide more comprehensive services, and be more consistent and reliable. Although it has been apparent to many major institutions that endowment is one way to attain financial stability, for most nonprofits endowment has only been a dream. The history of nonprofit fund raising is a history of needing money *now*. There is intense pressure on operating and capital monies.

Today things are changing. More and more nonprofits are stabilizing their financial situation by building endowment. Endowment fund raising is the hottest topic in the field of philanthropy. Leading national foundations such as Kresge and Ford have initiated major endowment projects across the country. Community Foundations are providing technical and investment support for nonprofits in endowment fund raising. In some cities, United Way has endowment projects designed to support its annual operations, and regional foundations such as the Rose Foundation in Denver have made a significant commitment to helping agencies and organizations build endowment.

Endowment is not the solution to every financial problem that the nonprofit has. In fact, the ordinary fund raising of the organization will have to continue aggressively, even with an endowment in place. Endowment can be the strong building block of financial stability.

Audience for This Workbook

This workbook is for development professionals who must take responsibility for the development of endowment in their organizations. It is also designed to help executive directors and others in charge of nonprofits understand the scope and scale of thinking and activity required by a commitment to raising endowment. Volunteer leaders of endowment efforts may also find sections of this book particularly helpful. My approach is to assume that your organization has had enough development experience to be familiar with basic fund raising terms and with general fund raising practices.

Goals of This Workbook

This workbook will provide you with a blueprint for building an endowment program. It will keep you from making the ordinary mistakes that are often made in the endowment arena. Even if you are simply exploring the possibility of endowment fund raising, this workbook will help you gather and analyze information.

You'll learn

- Ways to determine whether your organization can raise endowment

- Logical and systematic approaches to developing an endowment fund raising program

- An understanding of the strategic choices an institution faces when developing endowments

- An understanding that the secret to successful endowment fund raising is that *there is no secret* (any good fund raising organization can raise endowment)

- An approach to soliciting endowment donors that has worked successfully for other organizations

- An understanding of the unique components of endowment and what makes it different from other kinds of fund raising

What Is Covered

Chapter One defines *endowment*, explores its benefits, and describes the basic ways in which endowment is organized and managed. Assessing your organization's readiness for endowment fund raising is the focus of Chapter Two. In Chapter Three, I discuss volunteer and staff leadership, with recruitment ideas and solid principles of volunteer management. Chapter Four gets you started on building the internal and external systems that support endowment—budgets, for example. The essential steps of identifying, cultivating, and soliciting prospects are covered in Chapter Five. Chapter Six focuses on maintaining a strong relationship with the donor after the gift.

I do not provide information on investment practices with endowed funds, though I do offer suggestions for where to find this information in the Recommended Resources section of the book.

How to Use This Workbook

This is a workbook. It is short on narrative and long on worksheets. The workbook format allows you to apply the ideas and concepts presented therein to your organization. Everyone who uses this workbook will use it differently. The approach to endowment fund raising must be customized to your organization. Completing this workbook will help you help others in the critical decision making and planning so essential to successful fund raising for endowment.

Many chapters offer a step-by-step approach to the tasks necessary for building a successful endowment fund raising program. The *preparation* for endowment fund raising is discussed in some detail. Preparation may seem slow and tedious, but failure to prepare effectively and professionally will lead to time-consuming and unnecessary problems.

The Legacy of Hank Rosso

This workbook owes a great debt to the fund raising philosophy and teaching of Henry A. Rosso. Hank Rosso was the founder of the Fund Raising School and was the most eminent fund raising educator of the past century. As a professional, I grew up working with and learning from Hank Rosso. His views, approaches, and perspectives on fund raising infuse this workbook. Concepts such as organizational readiness, donor-centered fund raising, and stewardship are directly based on the ideas and values of the Rosso approach.

Hank Rosso would readily recognize the approach taken by this workbook, as it replicates the famous "Fund Raising Cycle" that he taught and that is now being taught in the Fund Raising School. The fund raising cycle describes a set of activities needed to prepare for and implement any kind of fund raising. There are fourteen steps in the cycle, as reflected in a diagram often used by the Fund Raising School and illustrated in the front of this book. Used with discipline and intelligence, these steps can ensure that your fund raising program will be effective.

Endowment building fits nicely into the Rosso model. The exercises in this workbook walk you though almost all the steps in the fund raising cycle. The following steps from Rosso's comprehensive listing of the cycle steps are used throughout this workbook:

- *Examine the case:* Making a strong case for the need for endowment is a critical component of successful endowment fund raising.

- *Define your objectives:* What will endowment do for your organization? What do you want it to do? Will the impact of endowment affect the lives of many people?

- *Involve volunteers:* There have been few successful endowment fund raising programs without strong volunteer leadership and involvement.

- *Select fund raising vehicles:* Endowment fund raising is a very personal kind of fund raising. The vehicles selected must reflect the personal approach.

- *Identify potential giving sources:* Identifying prospects for endowment giving is a great challenge for most organizations.

- *Prepare a fund raising plan:* Endowment fund raising gains greatly from a carefully drafted plan with clearly defined goals.

- *Prepare a communications plan:* Everyone must know about your endowment fund raising effort. Secret fund raising is never successful.

- *Solicit the gift:* It is in this activity that a very specific difference emerges for most nonprofits. The asking activity, done well, is critical to success.

- *Renew the gift:* Donors often make more than one endowment gift, so stewardship is crucial. Donor recognition plays a critical part in obtaining gift renewals.

Acknowledgments

I owe a considerable debt to Hank Rosso, the Fund Raising School, and the Center on Philanthropy at Indiana University for the inspiration, education, and opportunities that have been offered to me. In addition, the Fund Raising School faculty members with whom I have trained have been a constant source of encouragement and wonderful models of skilled and inspired professionals. I am also grateful to the Kresge Foundation and the Rose Foundation, both of which offered me the opportunity to be involved in nationally influential and innovative endowment pilot projects. "For Good, Forever" is one of the themes of the Kresge initiatives. I can't think of a better way to describe the powerful impact of the growth of endowment in nonprofit organizations across the country.

Seattle, Washington   Edward C. Schumacher
December 2002

The Author

EDWARD C. SCHUMACHER is president of Third Sector Consulting—a Seattle-based consulting firm that provides workshops and consultation to local, regional, national, and international nonprofit organizations. Before starting his own business in 1985, Schumacher had been an executive director, a development director, and a national staff member for nonprofit organizations in Maryland, New York, Colorado, and the state of Washington for twenty-five years. At the University of Washington, Schumacher helped found the nonprofit fund raising certificate program and was an instructor in the program for fifteen years. Currently, he serves as lead instructor for the Fund Raising School—a program of the Center on Philanthropy at Indiana University. During the past ten years, Schumacher has worked on three national pilot programs in endowment fund raising. He has published two books on capital campaigns: *The Capital Campaign Survival Guide* (Elton-Wolf, 1999) and *Capital Campaigns* (National Center for NonProfit Boards, 2000).

BUILDING
YOUR
ENDOWMENT

CHAPTER 1

Understanding Endowment

ENDOWMENT FUND RAISING differs from other fund raising in fundamental ways and offers distinct advantages to nonprofit organizations. But endowment fund raising should not to be entered into lightly. In this chapter, you will become familiar with the basic language of endowment fund raising and learn about the structural models that can be used to organize an endowment fund raising program. These tools are the basis of the education you and your organization's board and staff will need in order to make critical decisions about endowment fund raising.

DEFINITIONS

Endowment: A fund of money, the principal of which is held in perpetuity and invested and from which an organization may use only the return on investment.

Endowment fund: The formal term to describe the accounting placement of endowment monies in the income statement of an organization.

Endowment campaign: A campaign to raise endowment that is managed and directed much like a capital campaign, with specific goals and a time-limited framework.

Endowment program: The permanent, continuous fund raising effort to build endowment. From time to time, the program may include an endowment campaign.

Endowment advisory committee: A group that explores key questions about an organization's mission, structure, and donor base and evaluates its readiness for endowment building.

Endowment steering committee: The group of volunteers, both board members and nonboard members, whom the advisory committee selects to be responsible for a particular endowment fund raising effort.

Constituency: The group of potential donors to whom the endowment fund raising program is directed or marketed.

Unique Characteristics of Endowment Fund Raising

The strategies used to cultivate and solicit endowment gifts are similar to those used for major and capital gifts. But to build a successful endowment program, you'll need to be mindful of what's special about endowment fund raising:

The total raised will consist of a few large gifts rather than many small gifts. For the interest from an endowment to make a financial impact, there must be a significant amount of money in the endowment fund. The Rosso model, which suggests that 20 percent of the gifts should provide 80 percent of the dollars, applies to an endowment fund.

Negotiating an endowment gift will take longer than any other kind of fund raising. Because a request for an endowment gift often involves negotiating a major or planned gift, the time you spend with prospective donors will be longer and more demanding than the time you spend soliciting an annual gift or even a capital gift.

Endowment donors are sophisticated about ways of giving. Most donors have already been approached by their church, their college or university, or their hospital about endowment giving and planned giving. They know the language and often understand the nature of the gifts long before we call on them.

Solicitations will require you to make more personal contact than you do during other types of fund raising. Endowment fund raising can't be done entirely by phone or mail. The personal approach is the most effective because of the types of gifts requested and the complex nature of endowment.

Prospects will ask tough questions. Prospects will want to know where the money is invested, who the investment counsel will be, and what return you are expecting; they'll ask for a wide range of financial and money management information that is almost never requested during other kinds of fund raising.

Prospects will want proof that the endowment gift is a good investment. Balanced budgets, sound financial management, and board oversight of funds are all-important components of the endowment story. Prospects may well base their decisions on this information. They are making an investment; they think like investors.

Prospects will want proof that their endowment gift will make a difference. It is vital that your organization have a clear vision of the impact that endowment will have on the quality and quantity of service provided to the community by a nonprofit organization.

Prospects will want to know the entire endowment plan. They'll probably want to know how big the endowment will be, how many donors you expect, and what the long-term goal is. Endowment donors think big and ask tough questions. Your organization must have the answers.

The Benefits of Endowment

Endowment income provides key benefits to a nonprofit organization; these are discussed next.

Financial Stability

The nonprofit funding environment is volatile and creates a sense of unease and inconsistency. Income from endowment can effectively smooth out the rough spots in a fiscal year. Endowment can be used to underwrite programs that have not been funded, support budgets when there are shortfalls, enable management to continue to move the institution forward, even in difficult financial times, and provide a safety net when an unexpected financial crisis occurs. In sum, endowment can help an organization realize its inspirational and visionary ideas.

Use of Risk Capital

In the planning process, new and innovative programs and services are often discounted because they can't be funded. With income from endowment, organizations can take some risks. Endowed institutions can fund new programs, start new initiatives, and reach out to provide more services. Although such risk capital sometimes comes from generous donors, sources of that type are neither reliable nor consistent.

Financial Control

Virtually every source of nonprofit income, from earned income to philanthropic income, has been difficult to forecast. There are good years and bad years. There are variables in the environment that the nonprofit cannot control; donors, grantors, and even clients do not or cannot always do what we would like them to do financially. Income from endowment, however, is in the control of the organization; unrestricted endowment, in particular, becomes a bedrock of security and power for the organization. These types of endowment are described later in the chapter.

Donor Incentive

The existence of an endowment fund is an incentive for donors to give to an organization, because an organization with an endowment is likely to be perceived as stable and financially mature.

Permanence and Longevity

A prospective donor must believe and see evidence that an investment in endowment will continue to make a difference beyond the donor's lifetime. The very existence of the endowment is an important piece of evidence. When a donor sees a strong endowment, he or she understands that the organization will continue to exist for a long time.

Ten Reasons Why People Give to Endowment

Donors like to give to endowments for many of the same reasons they give to any cause they care about. However, you will find in the list that follows some reasons that are distinctly different from reasons for giving to anything else:

1. They believe in the cause, and they were asked to give.

2. They believe in the cause and have a link to it.

3. They believe in the asker.

4. They like the idea of perpetuity, that is, giving beyond their own life.

5. They are dedicated to the specific project or program with the organization that the endowment will fund.

6. Their business or industry will gain from the gift.

7. They like the idea that their gift will grow with sound investment and spending practices.

8. They are impressed with the investment advice and proposed management of the endowment.

9. They would rather give to your organization than to the government. In other words, they want the tax advantage.

10. They have a history of giving to endowment and understand the benefits.

Endowment Types

Every organization has some special financial needs and responsibilities that can be secured through endowment. Colleges and universities will always want scholarship funds for worthy students; hospitals will always want to underwrite the financial cost of care for those who cannot afford care, and other nonprofits will always want to underwrite specific institutional needs. And to help fill some of those needs, here are some of the many types of endowment to choose from:

Term endowment: A fund of money given by a donor to be used for a term agreed to by the nonprofit and the donor. For example, the donor may want the return on investment to be used for building maintenance and upkeep for a period of ten years, at which time the organization may use the principal as it sees fit.

Quasi-endowment: A fund from which the organization may take either the annual return or some portion of the principal for use as needed.

Unrestricted endowment: A gift that allows the institution the flexibility to use the return on investment as best serves the immediate needs of the institution.

Restricted Endowments

Another type of endowment is restricted gifts, which are somewhat more complicated in that the donor can choose to endow a specific program or a particular staff or faculty position; or the gift may fund an organization's recurring need. Restricted endowment gifts are attractive to many donors and can stabilize an organization. For example, if a donor endows the office of the symphony director and all attendant costs, any part of the symphony's operating budget that had originally been allocated to those costs is now available to be used as needed.

Here are some possibilities for restricted endowments:

Program endowment: A gift to a particular program within an organization that helps secure its future. For example, a health care institution may wish to endow the building and operating costs of a hospice, or a boys' and girls' club may wish to endow a basketball program.

Named memorial endowment: An endowment fund named for an individual being honored by the donor. For example, the Ralph Williams Endowed Fund may have been named by the children of Ralph Williams to honor his long affiliation with a school's athletic program.

Scholarship endowment: A fund that endows scholarships. Educational institutions have found that many donors wish to underwrite scholarship funds in perpetuity. Or a ballet company with a school or a social service agency that provides an educational component may find a scholarship endowment to be very helpful.

Uncompensated care endowment: A fund that allows donors to underwrite those who are least able to use the services of an organization. Such a fund could be particularly useful to children's hospitals, which often provide a great deal of uncompensated care.

Endowment for a faculty or staff chair: A fund that underwrites the cost of academic faculty through endowed chairs.

Facilities endowment: A gift to underwrite operating expenses. Fund raising for the day-to-day costs of heat, light, water, and power is exceedingly difficult. An endowment gift to underwrite these costs often comes from donors during a capital campaign.

Buildings and grounds endowment: A gift to underwrite the maintenance of property. Buildings and grounds always pose high financial risks to nonprofits. The ability to underwrite the cost of maintenance, repairs, and renovations through endowment stabilizes operational budgets.

Staff scholarship endowment: A gift to support education. For example, hospitals have had a great deal of success with building endowments to underwrite the cost of continuous and permanent nursing education.

Technology upgrade endowment: A gift to support improvements in technology. Technology changes so rapidly that no sooner does an organization update its technology than the technology becomes obsolete. For this reason, an endowment dedicated to helping an organization update and upgrade its technology continuously can be a most valuable gift.

Client services endowment: A gift to fund a service. A homeless shelter calculated that it would take $12,000 a year to operate one of its units for a family of four. The shelter set out to find six $10,000-endowment donors who, by combining their monies, would ensure that the shelter space was always available to a family. Donors loved the idea and found the size of the gift within reason. The joint venture worked quite successfully.

Integrating Endowment into Your Fund Raising Program

To be successful, an endowment program must be part of your organization's comprehensive fund raising plan. It is essential that fund raising for endowment be fed by the efforts of annual funds and the major gifts program. Successful endowment fund raising efforts are those that boast an ongoing, year-round process of cultivation, solicitation, and recognition; a permanent staff member usually oversees a successful endowment program. The staff person must make endowment fund raising a priority within the organization while educating the community about the importance of endowment.

It is easy to include an endowment fund when planning your general fund raising program. You might integrate endowment into your planned giving program by either establishing an endowment fund and soliciting planned gifts specifically for this fund or by creating named endowment funds as part of the planned giving process. You may choose to solicit endowment gifts the way you would annual gifts—asking for current cash or cash-equivalent gifts through face-to-face meetings or special mailings and directing the funds into the endowment. Many organizations choose to include an endowment fund raising element in a capital campaign, thus raising money to build a facility and funds to ensure its long-term use and maintenance at the same time.

Endowment Structures and Planned Giving

It is crucial that the organization and its donors understand that planned giving is not endowment any more than endowment is planned giving. The former is a type of fund, and the latter is a fund raising vehicle. Planned giving actually encompasses several giving vehicles, such as charitable remainder trusts, life insurance, and wills. The money from these planned gifts is often used to create and fund endowments. Donors may give cash, securities, property, and other tangible items that have a dollar value to an endowment fund. Planned giving is often considered the most efficient and effective way to raise money for endowment.

Organization–Owned Endowment

A nonprofit organization may choose to integrate an endowment fund and fund raising program into its current organizational structure. In this case, endowment staff is part of the fund raising staff. The day-to-day management of endowment is done in the financial offices of the organization, and day-to-day endowment fund raising looks and acts like simply an additional kind of organizational fund raising. The benefits of this model are efficiency and clarity of roles and responsibilities. For prospective and established donors, this model has the benefit of raising no questions about who is in charge of what.

However, care must be taken that the establishment of this endowment structure is not simply a formality. If the seams show, if the organization is on overload, if staff have no room left for an additional task, if endowment fund raising is just another item on the to-do list of already burdened board members, then this model will not work.

Separate Foundation

Some organizations choose to establish a separate and independent 501(c)3 organization to secure, manage, and distribute endowment. This organization is sometimes called a foundation, although it does not meet the true definition of a foundation, which is tied to the organization through bylaws, articles of incorporation, and the practice of linked boards. The foundation has a separate board with its own bylaws, articles, and operating practices, but board members often come in part or entirely from the founding organization. Key components of this organizational relationship include staffing, investing, allocating annual returns, using the organizational logo and name, and marketing.

There are good reasons for the establishment of a separate endowment-holding foundation. In some organizations, the board members have no responsibility for private sector fund raising and, frankly, no interest in it. Furthermore, in some organizations the day-to-day demands of operations and fund raising are so overwhelming that the addition of yet another function, without a separate supporting entity, would be impractical and could bring the whole system crashing down. Under these circumstances, if an endowment is to be created, a separate entity to raise and manage funds must be created as well.

Finally, an endowment foundation might be established because it enables the organization to identify, select, and recruit power brokers in the community. In terms of status, there is no comparison between being on an endowment committee and sitting on a foundation board. It may well be determined that the only way to get the "right" people involved is to have a structure that seems to offer them the status and stature they require.

The two models discussed next—Community Foundations and umbrella funds—are particularly appropriate for small nonprofits just starting to build endowments.

Community Foundations

If a nonprofit does not wish to form its own foundation, it may choose to associate with a Community Foundation. Community Foundations are established under a special set of federal laws that provide for only one organization of a particular type in a given community. Thus an organization has the privilege of being the only one of its kind in a given community.

Today, most Community Foundations across the country have both the capacity and the willingness to manage endowment funds for nonprofit organizations. The Community Foundation has the capacity to combine the endowment funds of many nonprofits, thus getting a big return at a low cost. Community Foundations are attractive to donors because they often have a long track record of investment success.

However, you may encounter resistance to the idea of turning over fund investment management to a Community Foundation. Often the funds become the property of the Community Foundation, and the principal will be returned only under a set of agreed-to circumstances. Boards in particular have some difficulty with giving up control of the endowment principal. Although it is true that the funds are in the control of the Community Foundation, the reality is that the funds were never flexible in the first place. They cannot be spent or used in any way. The credibility of the Community Foundation and its skills in investing are what the nonprofit is trading for perceived control.

National Umbrellas

Some national nonprofit organizations have set up umbrella organizations to hold endowments for local chapters or affiliates. If you are a member agency or affiliate, you will find your money in a large investment fund with the chances of both a better return and a lower cost than if you invested on your own.

What's Next?

Now that you are familiar with some of the basic concepts of endowment, you are ready to help your organization do an initial exploration of its commitment to and readiness for an endowment-building effort.

Assessing Your Readiness

ENDOWMENT IS NOT for every organization. For example, your institution may be too small or too young to begin endowment fund raising. This chapter will help your organization determine whether you are ready to go about creating and building an endowment fund. The worksheets will help you develop the information you need to make informed decisions.

Forming the Endowment Advisory Committee

The first step in assessing your organization's readiness for an endowment fund raising effort is for the board to appoint the *endowment advisory committee*—a thoughtful group of volunteers and staff—to explore key questions about issues such as your organization's mission, structure, and donor base as they relate to endowment building. Look for people in the organization who have experience with and know the importance of endowment.

The endowment advisory committee's job is to ensure that management and development staff members are educated about endowment fund raising and to determine whether endowment is right for your organization at this time. The committee might include the executive director, board chair, finance chair, past board chair, development director, and financial officer. All of these individuals share a knowledge of the financial state of the nonprofit, of the community, and of the constituency. In addition, the volunteers engaged should have a fairly wide understanding of the community being served and the financial resources of that community. The combined knowledge of the group will enable them to make effective decisions and recommendations to the board.

Worksheet 2.1 enables you to define the qualities you are looking for in endowment advisory committee members and use those criteria to select a final group.

WORKSHEET 2.1

Creating Your Endowment Advisory Committee

Once you've identified the qualities you are looking for in endowment advisory committee members, you can create an initial list from which the board can select the final members.

List the attributes, skills, and characteristics you are seeking:

_____

_____

_____

_____

_____

Prospective Members   **Final Selection**

1. _____   1. _____

2. _____   2. _____

3. _____   3. _____

4. _____   4. _____

5. _____   5. _____

6. _____

7. _____

8. _____

9. _____

10. _____

The rest of this chapter discusses in detail the kinds of information that would be useful for the endowment advisory committee to gather.

Evaluating and Building Commitment

No endowment fund raising effort can be successful without the basic commitment of key people and resources within the organization. So one of the advisory committee's first tasks should be to evaluate the commitment level within your organization.

Board Commitment

One important indicator of potential board commitment to endowment is its involvement in your organization's current activities. Has the board played an active role in governing the organization, in planning, defining, approving, and clarifying policy, in overseeing management resources, and in generating resources through fund raising? Use Worksheet 2.2 to assess your organization's current level of board leadership.

Building board support for an endowment-building effort is not always easy, because along with all the powerful benefits of endowment comes a substantial burden of financial responsibility. Board members quickly become aware that they will have to give to endowment and raise funds for endowment as part of their commitment. And the board is responsible for the care of the endowment. The efforts of the board must meet very high standards—consistently and over long periods of time. In a *Journal of Accountancy* article titled "The Endowment Goose and Its Golden Eggs" published in September 1995, Susan L. Prenatt relates the origin of these standards:

> The legal standard of fiduciary responsibility applicable to trustees of endowed institutions comes from a 1830 case, Harvard College v. Amory. Known as the prudent man rule, it requires a trustee to "observe how men of prudence . . . manage their own affairs . . . considering the probably [sic] income as well as the probably [sic] safety of the capital to be invested." [p. 66]

Each board member must be able and willing to take on this fiduciary responsibility.

Commitment of Staff and Resources

Whether your organization has sufficient staff, time, and money for an endowment program depends on the size of the organization and the scope of the proposed endowment. One can run an endowment program with as little as a quarter-time staff member, a $15,000 budget, and a small committee of volunteers.

Use Worksheet 2.3 to determine whether there is currently sufficient support for endowment among the leaders of your organization and whether sufficient resources could be allocated to an endowment-building effort.

WORKSHEET 2.2

Board Leadership

Endowment fund raising demands an assessment of all the resources of the organization, including the human resources. This worksheet enables you to candidly assess the board. Use it as part of the readiness and planning process for the endowment initiative. In a confidential setting, you might also want to use it with the executive director and the board chair.

1. How would you describe the board of your organization?

   ☐ Movers and shakers of the community

   ☐ Hardworking, but mostly unknown

   ☐ A few leaders, the rest followers

2. What is the board's present level of participation in the organization's annual fund?

   _____%

3. What is the board's present level of participation in the organization's most recent capital fund drive?

   _____%

4. How many board members have named the organization in their wills or indicated a willingness to do so?

   _____%

5. Which statement best characterizes the board's support of the organization's major giving or planned giving program?

   ☐ Three or more board members have made endowment gifts.

   ☐ Most board members would be receptive to making an endowment gift.

   ☐ Five or more board members will solicit friends and peers.

WORKSHEET 2.3

Commitment of the Board, Staff, and Resources to Endowment Fund Raising

This worksheet will give you and the endowment advisory committee a place to start thinking about your organization's commitment to endowment. Don't embark on an endowment fund raising effort until the answer to all these questions is yes.

Board Commitment

1. Is the board supportive of the concept of endowment?

   ☐ Yes   ☐ No

2. If not, can we effectively address the board's objections and questions?

   ☐ Yes   ☐ No

3. Strategy:

   _____

   _____

   _____

   _____

4. Are there individuals available (board members, volunteers) capable of leading the charge?

   ☐ Yes   ☐ No

5. If so, name at least three of these individuals:

   _____   _____   _____

6. Will staff members involved in the effort have access to the board?

   ☐ Yes   ☐ No

WORKSHEET 2.3 (continued)

Staff Commitment

1. Who will oversee the endowment fund raising effort? How much time will that staff member spend on endowment gifts? What other responsibilities must that person fulfill?

_____

_____

_____

_____

_____

2. Will the person responsible for the endowment program have administrative support?

   ☐ Yes   ☐ No

3. Who will conduct research on prospects for endowment gifts?

   _____   _____   _____

   _____   _____   _____

Commitment of Resources

1. Does the organization have adequate financial resources to manage an endowment fund raising program?

   ☐ Yes   ☐ No

2. Has the organization provided funds for training the staff and cultivating donors?

   ☐ Yes   ☐ No

Developing the Case Statement

The case for endowment fund raising differs from other case statements in that it speaks about the long-term future as well as the present. A written statement of case, needs, and goals that is *specifically tailored to endowment* allows you to determine all the reasons why anyone should give. This document can be used to enlist the support of those within the organization and engage the interest of prospective donors. The organization's case for endowment fund raising can

- Outline the ways in which endowment will support the mission and vision of the organization
- Talk about how endowment can help the organization meet the needs of its constituency
- Address financial stability in a difficult time
- Propose that the permanence of the organization depends on endowment

As with all fund raising, a strong statement of need is not only invaluable; it is necessary. Use Worksheet 2.4 to begin to construct your organization's endowment case statement. Once you have created the case statement, board, staff, and other key leaders within the organization should be able to express the case in exciting terms that communicate their own commitments.

Sample Case Statement

The following sample case statement meets most of the requirements of a simple, well-written, and clearly defined statement of rationale.

> The Willows Run Senior Home provides services to low-income seniors in the community of Valley Dale. For forty-five years, the Home has treated seniors with dignity and kindness regardless of financial resources. We believe every individual has a right to food, shelter, and health care in their golden years.
>
> The Willows Run Senior Home is embarking on an endowment-building program to stabilize the financial resources of the organization. Tough economic times and difficult financial markets greatly affect the organization. Fewer people can be served, and at times even service compromises have to be made. This is unacceptable. The income from a carefully invested endowment will provide a consistent flow of dollars to help underwrite difficult times and, in good times, to help develop new and innovative programs for seniors.
>
> Your gift to the Willows Run Endowment fund will be managed by prudent financial experts and will have an effect on the lives of seniors and the quality of life in our community forever. Consider making your gift today.

WORKSHEET 2.4

Building the Case for Endowment

Now's the time to begin building your case for endowment fund raising. Answering the questions that follow will guide your thinking as to whether your organization is truly ready.

1. What is the value of your organization in the community?

   _____

   _____

2. What are the values that your organization stands for?

   _____

   _____

3. Describe the impact of endowment income on your organization's services.

   Qualitative: (Will something be better?)

   _____

   _____

   _____

   Quantitative: (Will more of something be done?)

   _____

   _____

   _____

4. Identify three benefits of endowment to your organization:

   _____

   _____

   _____

WORKSHEET 2.4 (continued)

5. How will endowment income support, expand, or help your mission?

_____

_____

_____

6. What is the long-term value of endowment to your organization?

_____

_____

_____

Once the endowment advisory committee has determined that the commitment of leaders and resources is in place and you have a preliminary case statement, it is time to do an assessment of how well your organization is currently prepared to take on an endowment-building effort.

Cornerstones of Endowment Fund Raising

No endowment fund raising effort can move forward until a strong organizational foundation, consisting of the elements discussed next, is in place.

Strategic Plan

The organization's strategic plan is the blueprint of the future of the organization and needs to be in place before you even consider an endowment program. Endowment and the need for it should be woven throughout the strategic plan. Does your organization have a written strategic plan that charts its course for three (ideally five) years, starting with a statement of mission, goals, and objectives and then moving into specific programs and budgets? For example, the strategic plan of a university might call for new initiatives in science and technology. It should be clear that certain of the science and technology facilities, programs, and even faculty positions can be endowed to ensure future success. Endowment is designed to make the strategic plan possible.

Mission and Vision

The whole purpose of building endowment is to support the mission and vision of your organization. You need clear, concise, and powerful mission and vision statements that are supported by the actions of the organization if you are to be successful at *any* type of fund raising—but especially endowment fund raising. Endowment donors are really long-term investors who must be assured that you have a clear mission and a strong vision of the future in which they are investing. You want your organization, as well as its mission and vision, to be highly visible.

Fund Raising Program

A strong, well-organized fund raising program can easily integrate endowment fund raising into the organizational fund raising plans and initiatives. The organization needs, at the very least, a donor base, board members who give, and a development professional who can integrate endowment into the ongoing fund raising in the organization or oversee the creation of a foundation. Endowment fits into the scheme of fund raising that includes an annual fund, capital fund raising, major gifts, and planned giving; a planned gift program can actually support the growth of an endowment. Remember that big gifts generally come from donors who have made smaller gifts, and bigger gifts come from people who have made big gifts.

REAL-WORLD EXAMPLE

A small opera company was concerned that seeking endowment gifts from some of its benefactors might detract from their willingness to give their usual generous annual gift. Staff members came together prior to the endowment effort to develop tactics and strategies that would provide the opportunity for donors to give to both endowment and the annual fund. This might be done by focusing on planned gifts or gifts of stock or property for the endowment fund while continuing to send cash gifts for the annual fund. Thanks to this collaboration, the feeling of competition within the development office was diminished, donors were treated with great care, and many donors agreed to donate to both endowment and the annual fund.

Worksheet 2.5 provides some questions you and the endowment advisory committee should be asking about your organization's fund raising program.

Donor Base

The more your organization knows about its donor base, the better. Demographics are a vital factor in endowment fund raising. Although it is dangerous to generalize, the most likely donor to endowment is a person over

WORKSHEET 2.5

Analyzing Your Current Fund Raising Program

The older and more sophisticated your fund raising program is, the better chance you have of succeeding at endowment fund raising. The questions to follow should help you identify strengths and weaknesses; answering all the questions in the affirmative will be an indication that you are ready to begin endowment fund raising.

1. Does the organization have experience in attracting gift support for current programs (an annual fund) or for capital purposes? If yes, please list some examples.

   _____

   _____

   _____

2. Does this experience include raising major gifts? If yes, please list some examples.

   _____

   _____

   _____

3. Have the fund raising programs been directed to all market sources available—individuals, foundations, corporations, and associations? Please list examples from each of these four market source categories.

   _____

   _____

   _____

4. Is competent, qualified staff available to plan fund raising programs and to provide support to volunteers? Is this staff able to devote its full energy and time to the fund raising function? If yes, please list the names of these employees.

   _____   _____   _____

   _____   _____   _____

   _____   _____   _____

fifty years old. Another likely donor is a past board member. Those who maintain a connection with the organization are traditionally some of the best leaders in endowment fund raising and are the best donors themselves.

Worksheets 2.6 and 2.7 provide some questions you and the endowment advisory committee should be asking about your organization's donor base. Worksheet 2.7 will help you look more closely at your donor base and provide a few clues as to your readiness for endowment building. Although there are no exact rules, the more active donors, major gift donors, and older donors you have, the better your chances are for a successful endowment program.

More Important Factors in Endowment-Building Success

To expand its review, I strongly recommend that the advisory committee consider your organization's position with regard to the issues discussed in the sections that follow.

Ethical Practice

The endowment fund raising process often challenges organizations with complex ethical issues. To prepare for your endowment effort, your organization should construct a system for dealing with troublesome issues, questions of self-interest, and ethical reporting.

The nonprofit organization can obtain considerable help with thinking about issues of ethics from the professional sources within fund raising. All of the following have statements of professional ethics that should be reviewed: Association of Fundraising Professionals national and local chapters, American Association of Fund Raising Council, Evangelical Council for Financial Accountability, Council for the Advancement and Support of Education (college and university fund raisers), and the Association for Healthcare Philanthropy. All of these sources can provide explicit ethical information.

Age and Reputation

The older the organization, the better the chances for raising endowment. Older organizations generally have prospective donors who are old enough to be interested in endowment building. The organization's longevity brings with it the evidence of stability and assurance of continuation that these prospects look for. Prospective donors will look to the organization's reputation to determine whether they will give.

WORKSHEET 2.6

Historical Analysis of Your Donor Base

As with Worksheet 2.5, the questions here are designed to help you assess strengths and weaknesses and to set goals to reach that will enable you to give an affirmative answer to each.

1. Has research on donors (particularly at the major gift level) been conducted over the years? If no, what is needed to begin conducting such research?

_____

_____

_____

2. Is a donor record-keeping system in place that provides storage and retrieval of essential data in a timely fashion? Will the system support the acknowledgment of all contributions within forty-eight hours of receipt? If no, what is needed to establish and maintain such a system?

_____

_____

_____

_____

3. Are present donors considered a special constituency for communications, and is their involvement carefully developed through two-way communication? If no, what could be done to improve these communications?

_____

_____

_____

_____

Statistical Analysis of Your Donor Base

Because the most likely endowment donor is already a donor to your organization, it is vital to understand your existing donor base. This review of your donor base is primarily statistical, but it begins to point the way to prospective endowment donors.

1. How many active donors (in the last eighteen months) are in your file? _____
   Do you have donors at these levels of giving annually? How many?

   $500 to $1,000   _____
   $1,001 to $2,500   _____
   $2,501 to $5,000   _____
   $5,001 to $7,500   _____
   $7,501 to $10,000   _____

2. What is the cumulative giving of your top ten donors over the past five years?

   $5,000 to $10,000   _____
   $10,001 to $15,000   _____
   $15,001 to $20,000   _____
   $20,001 to $30,000   _____
   $30,001 to $50,000 or above   _____

4. What is the age range of your top ten donors?

   20 to 30   _____
   31 to 40   _____
   41 to 50   _____
   51 to 60   _____
   61 to 70   _____
   71 and above   _____

5. How many donors do you know who have already put you in their wills? _____

6. How many of your current board members are among the top ten donors? _____

7. What is the age range of the complete donor list (generally if not specifically)?
   31 to 40   _____
   41 to 50   _____
   51 to 60   _____
   61 to 70   _____
   71 and above   _____

Constituency

Has the organization defined a constituency beyond those "intimately and naturally" involved with its programs? Has it developed an outreach program to increase the size of the constituency? Has it analyzed the makeup of the constituency for endowment fund raising purposes? Is there a constituency-wide communications plan, soundly conceived and implemented, to involve people in a warm, supportive relationship with the organization and designed to develop acceptance of the organization within the community?

Financial Stability

Is there a history of balanced budgets, an ability to manage financial resources effectively, sound cash flow management, and good financial planning within your organization? All are essential to managing endowment fund raising.

Another Perspective

Your organization can benefit from talking with other nonprofits in your area that possess endowments to learn how they got started. You may also wish to seek outside, expert help from consultants and endowment fund raisers.

Now that you've given some thought to the many complex factors that contribute to an organization's readiness for endowment building, use Worksheet 2.8 to analyze how well your organization's current structure and activities prepare it for an endowment-building effort.

Worksheet 2.8 will help you see where your organization is and where you may need to improve before beginning an endowment program. You want to be able to answer yes to all the yes-no questions. The older your organization, the older your donors, and the more bequests and planned gifts you have, the better chance you have to succeed at endowment fund raising. However, an endowment can be started with one very generous donor who has only given annual gifts in the past, so just use the worksheet as a general guideline for creating goals.

WORKSHEET 2.8

Analyzing Your Organization's History

Gathering information about your organization's past and present activities will help you predict its capacity for endowment-building success in the future.

1. How old is the organization? _____

2. How old are the oldest members or constituents? _____

3. How many members or constituents are fifty years old or older? _____

4. Does the organization maintain a comprehensive list of names and addresses of members or constituents, business prospects, those served, and so on?

   ☐ Yes   ☐ No

5. Does the organization have a history of receiving large gifts from individuals, corporations, and foundations?

   ☐ Yes   ☐ No

6. How many bequests has the organization received in the past three years? _____

7. How many planned gifts does the organization have under contract? _____

8. What is the dollar amount of all current endowment funds? _____

9. Is there a program or system for keeping past board members involved with the organization?

   ☐ Yes   ☐ No

10. Are there comprehensive investment practices and policies?

    ☐ Yes   ☐ No

11. Are there vehicles (publications, and so on) for promoting endowment giving?

    ☐ Yes   ☐ No

12. Does the organization have a high level of acceptance and visibility in the community?

    ☐ Yes   ☐ No

13. Are the organization's values clearly stated in public documents?

    ☐ Yes   ☐ No

Conducting a Feasibility Study

If, after filling out the worksheets in this chapter, you and the endowment advisory committee still feel unsure of your organization's readiness or ability to create and manage an endowment, you may choose to conduct a feasibility study. This study can be focused on either a general endowment fund or an endowment campaign.

It is a conventional step for organizations to conduct some kind of feasibility study prior to any major fund raising initiative. An endowment feasibility study is simply the testing of ideas about the organization and endowment with a thoughtful and informed audience composed of people close to the organization who are willing to offer advice and candid opinions. The study is also a marketing tool because it informs people about the proposed endowment project and tests its validity.

Preparation for a feasibility study should be comprehensive enough to anticipate and address questions from prospective donors—questions such as these:

- Is there a need for endowment?

- How much endowment will be raised, over what period of time?

- What will the return on investment be used for?

- What impact will endowment make on clients, services, constituency, and finances? Will endowment be restricted?

- Why do endowment fund raising now?

- Who will manage the endowment and endowment funds?

A good endowment feasibility study addresses multiple questions, such as the following. Does the prospective donor

- Understand what endowment is?

- Demonstrate a belief in the concept of endowment for a nonprofit organization?

- Understand the organization's case for endowment?

- Support any or all of the programs or projects proposed to be funded by the endowment?

- Feel satisfied with the state of the organization and positive about its future?

- Accept as reasonable the endowment goal (dollars to be raised)?

- Demonstrate willingness to be involved in an endowment fund raising effort?

Study Models

There are several feasibility study models to choose from.

Traditional Feasibility Study

This is a study conducted by outside counsel, comprising a series of one-on-one confidential interviews with from thirty to one hundred prospective donors and leaders. It might also include focus groups and written questionnaires if there is a large constituency. Counsel and the organization jointly select the interviewees. The questionnaire is reviewed and revised as needed by the organization. Such a study can take from ninety to one hundred and twenty days, depending on variables such as the availability of interviewees. This is a costly exercise but one that brings a level of objectivity and outside perspective not offered by other feasibility study models.

In-House Study

An in-house study is much like a traditional feasibility study except that the person conducting it is a member of the organization's development staff. Although an insider-led study might mitigate the candor of some prospective donors, it can also give substantial insight into what people think, feel, and observe about the institution and endowment. The interviewer in this case will have his or her own personal experience with the organization and therefore a special perspective from which to interpret interviewees' comments.

Focus-Group Study

Focus groups should comprise donors, past donors, board members, friends of the organization, potential major benefactors, potential endowment volunteers, and some prospects for endowment fund raising. Group meetings might take the form of town hall meetings, with a major part of the constituency, or gatherings of six or fewer people in an intimate setting. Either hired counsel or development staff may lead the group.

Combination Studies

Some organizations take a comprehensive approach to studying feasibility, using one-on-one interviews, focus groups, and a mailed-out questionnaire to some portion of the constituency. Parts of this study may be conducted by outside counsel, with the development officer participating. This broad-based type of study often touches on more than the prospects for major gifts and the immediate family of the organization; it may include local politicians with an interest in the organization, well-known philanthropists, and foundation executives.

The feasibility study report should be confidential and submitted both orally and in written form. You may choose to create a separate summary report for wider distribution. The board should receive and formally accept the report. After reviewing the results with the endowment advisory committee, the board should authorize an endowment fund raising campaign. This action should be recorded in the minutes of the board meeting and become a permanent record of authorization.

What's Next?

You have now moved through a careful and deliberate review of the status of your organization and have concluded that moving forward with endowment fund raising is in the best interest of your organization. The endowment advisory committee should be the group to recruit the *permanent endowment steering committee* of the board to lead the fund raising effort. This group will be discussed in Chapter Three.

CHAPTER 3

Volunteer and Staff Leadership

IT GOES WITHOUT SAYING that causes do not raise money; people with causes raise money. The success or failure of the endowment effort will directly correlate with the quality of volunteer and staff leadership working on the project. This chapter will help you define the volunteer and staff roles in your endowment-building effort and find the right individuals to fill those roles.

Creating Endowment–Building Committees

Before an endowment program begins, the board needs to create certain committees to oversee the various aspects of the program. Committees are responsible to the board, though they may also work closely with staff. As committee members work together to achieve a common goal for your organization, they take ownership of and responsibility for the project while sharing the burdens and challenges of the work.

These committees are composed primarily of volunteers and are chaired by a volunteer, who may in some cases be a board member. The committees always have staff assigned as advisers to provide support and leadership. The chair and the committee look to staff for expertise and guidance in making choices.

Your endowment advisory committee, which you created in Chapter Two, will dissolve once it helps put permanent committees in place. Next are descriptions of (1) the permanent endowment steering committee that the advisory committee creates and (2) the investment committee, which is appointed by the finance committee of the board. Both are crucial to the effectiveness of endowment fund raising.

Endowment Steering Committee

This committee, which reports to the board, will be entrusted with the oversight and planning of the endowment fund raising program once it is in place. It becomes a standing committee that will meet regularly as needed. Members work with endowment staff to establish annual goals and benchmarks for endowment fund raising, review the work of the development staff, and advise when appropriate. As stewards of the endowment fund, they will make sure the funds are used in the most effective and efficient way possible and will assure donors that the endowment funds are being used exactly as directed.

This group will

- Determine endowment fund raising goals
- Help define the fund raising marketplace
- Review and accept written materials to be used in the endowment effort
- Help create a marketing plan
- Review and accept the case for endowment that the organization will use

A secondary role for the endowment steering committee is to operate individually as endowment fund raisers. This role includes

- Making their own endowment gift
- Identifying among friends and colleagues those who might be prospects
- Participating in the education and cultivation of prospects
- Being involved in the ask when appropriate
- Being involved in donor recognition, gift acknowledgment, and the thanking process
- Being involved in stewardship activities with past donors and those committed to endowment-by-bequest

The endowment advisory committee should use Worksheet 3.1 to determine the qualities desired in members of the endowment steering committee and use those criteria to select a final group.

Endowment Investment Committee

This also becomes a standing board committee; it is charged with the oversight of the endowment, its management, investment, distribution, and growth. This is not a fund raising committee per se but has a continuous responsibility for financial practices, even during the term of an endowment campaign effort. This group is responsible for ensuring the protection of the

WORKSHEET 3.1
Creating Your Endowment Committee

Once you've identified the qualities you are looking for in endowment committee members you can create an initial list from which the board can select the final members.

List the attributes, skills, and characteristics you are seeking:

_____

_____

_____

_____

_____

Prospective Members   **Final Selection**

1. _____   1. _____

2. _____   2. _____

3. _____   3. _____

4. _____   4. _____

5. _____   5. _____

6. _____

7. _____

8. _____

9. _____

10. _____

endowment. Members must carefully select counsel to invest the endowment funds, see to it that there is regular and consistent reporting on the investment portfolio, and schedule an annual audit of the investments and investment practices.

What to Look for in Staff and Volunteers

The first goal in building an endowment leadership team is to find the right people. Those experienced in endowment fund raising indicate that the most successful endowment efforts are collaborations between volunteers and staff members who possess certain characteristics, skills, and attitudes. Volunteer and staff leaders should hold some of the following values and views in common:

- A deep and abiding conviction about the value of the cause and the organization

- A belief in endowment and the benefits of endowment to the organization

- A willingness to be part of a team working on endowment

- A personal giving commitment to the endowment

Each volunteer and staff member should also share some of the following attributes:

- An understanding of planned giving and planned giving instruments

- An understanding of financial planning

- An understanding of financial assets and their uses in philanthropy

- An understanding of investment practices and choices in investing

- An understanding of the law as it relates to endowment giving, planned gift instruments, and financial management

- A level of comfort dealing with financial matters

- A willingness to find prospects for the endowment effort

- A willingness to cultivate and educate prospective donors

- A willingness to ask for the gift

- A respect for the power of charitable giving in someone's life

You will seldom find one person who possesses all the skills and characteristics listed here, but the endowment effort will move more effectively toward success if many of these characteristics and skills are present in the ranks of the endowment leadership.

Defining Roles and Responsibilities

You need to be prepared to provide potential volunteers and staff with some basic information about the effort they are about to undertake. The specifics will be driven by the size and scale of your organization, the size and scale of the fund raising effort, and the traditional ways of work in the organization.

Here are some guidelines for creating a well-conceived and well-defined job:

Keep it simple. The organizational chart should be easily understood and easily explained.

Define accountability. Everyone wants to know what they are expected to accomplish. Be outcome-focused with job and task descriptions.

Recognize the chain of command. The final word on all matters of policy related to endowment belongs to the board and to the committees it creates. The final say in the management and the day-to-day administration of the endowment belongs to staff, who should take volunteer advice into account as appropriate.

Define closure. Decide when the committee is expected to be done with its work. No volunteer wants an open-ended assignment.

Define relationships with staff. Which staff members will work with and support the volunteer group?

Here is a simple tool to use in the education of volunteers and staff about who does what in an endowment fund raising effort. This tool can allay confusion and confirm both volunteer and staff jobs.

Board	Staff
Prospecting	Prospecting
Education	Education
Cultivation	Cultivation
Giving	Giving
Asking	Asking*
Thanking	Thanking
	Managing
	Planning
	Training

---

*Only as a secondary asker

Selecting and Recruiting

Now that you have some guidelines on what to look for in volunteers and staff members and in how to define the job for them, you are ready to select and recruit particular individuals. Here are a couple of ways to start the search:

Inside Out

The key leaders for an endowment effort are already involved in the organization. They may be current or past board members, boosters, friends, current or past donors, major benefactors, or others with a close connection to the organization. It may be essential to rebuild some bridges to persons who once were close to the organization but have drifted away.

This initiative is the perfect reason to call past board members and supporters and get them together, to meet with them in small groups, to reconnect them with the organization. There may well be among them the leadership, expertise, and vision that are essential to your success. People who do not know the organization, regardless of their stature, prestige, or financial resources, should not be in your first tier of prospects. However, such people can be cultivated for leadership roles over time.

Upside Down

Start at the top of the leadership structure in your organization. Are the people currently in leadership the right people to lead the endowment-building effort? Sometimes they are and sometimes they are not. Don't overlook them because they currently have a high level of responsibility. Jobs and people can be interchanged. The new endowment initiative might be just the right medicine to rejuvenate leadership.

Potential volunteer leaders should be recruited and asked to serve by other volunteer leaders. Some staff might also be engaged in the recruitment, but volunteers who are peers have the best chance of making a successful recruitment. The recruiter also has to know how to describe the case for endowment that you developed in Chapter Two and the needs of the organization. This will not be an easy recruitment. Not everyone is interested in endowment, and an honest recruitment will deter some people from serving. Be prepared to be turned down, and pursue only those people who show some enthusiasm for the project. These are the people likely to know the job and understand its demands.

Working Practices with Volunteers

Keeping volunteers happily engaged in an endowment fund raising initiative takes particularly sensitive staff and volunteer leaders. Endowment fund raising is not quick, and it is not quickly gratifying; relationships with prospective donors last a long time. In addition, volunteers have a great deal of homework and preparation for endowment fund raising, so do what you can to make the volunteer's job fun, achievable, and gratifying. Here are some strategies for helping volunteers succeed in endowment fund raising:

Don't have any more meetings than are absolutely necessary. Guard volunteer time. It does not require a meeting for two people to talk to each other while others watch. Get those two together without everyone else.

Meetings should not exceed ninety minutes. Time is the most valuable asset, and work should be efficient as well as effective. Meetings should be carefully planned and very productive. If brainstorming and creative thinking are required, set aside a retreat time for that activity.

Create tasks that are time-limited and clearly defined. For example, give a key volunteer the names of two prospects to cultivate and educate. A list of ten or even five may be overwhelming.

Honor effort as well as outcomes. Sometimes a volunteer will work long and hard with a prospect to no avail. That volunteer often is bypassed when it comes to recognition because he or she did not make a gift happen. However, the effort was substantial, and the volunteer should be thanked and respected for it.

Respect the volunteer for what he or she brings to the process. Not everyone will be a good asker, but some might have a substantial body of knowledge about prospects, some might have great contacts, and others might be savvy cultivators of prospective donors. Make sure the assignments fit the volunteers.

Have clearly defined measures of success. Enable volunteers to know when they are doing well. Reinforce the good work they do with recognition and informal thanks.

Recognize volunteers. Have an ongoing, active volunteer recognition program.

Use Worksheet 3.2 to make the decisions that will enable you to clearly and effectively communicate your expectations to volunteers and staff.

Once the selected staff and volunteers are in place, the real work can begin. What follows is a description of the general tasks undertaken by the different people likely to find themselves either on or working closely with the endowment steering committee. The tools of their work will be discussed in greater detail in the remaining chapters.

WORKSHEET 3.2

Defining What's Expected of Volunteers and Staff

Use this worksheet as you get ready to recruit volunteers. Be sure that you and other recruiters can answer these questions for prospective leaders. A good job of recruiting signals an organization ready to make the best use of volunteer time and skills.

1. Agreement on frequency of meetings

   How often will the whole group meet? _____

   _____

   How often will subcommittees meet? _____

   _____

2. Agreement on location of meetings

   Will meetings be in the office or out? _____

   _____

   Will the setting be formal or informal? _____

   _____

3. Agreement on length of meetings

   Will the initial meeting be longer than subsequent ones? _____

   _____

   Will certain meetings (for example, for reviews) be longer than others? _____

4. Agreement on the format for agenda planning

   Who sets the agenda? _____

   _____

   Who has the final say on agenda items? _____

   _____

WORKSHEET 3.2 (continued)

5. Agreement on the format for minutes

   Does the organization have a standard format? _____

   _____

6. Agreement on subcommittee structure

   How many subgroups will be needed? _____

   _____

   Is a chair needed for each group? _____

   _____

7. Agreement on the definition of staff role in the committee

   Is more than one staff member involved? _____

   _____

   How do their roles relate to each other? _____

   _____

8. Agreement on the style or method of running the meetings

   Does the organization follow a standard for all its committees? _____

   _____

9. Agreement on expectations for committee members in addition to meetings

   Are members expected to attend other events? _____

   _____

   Are members expected to solicit donations? _____

   _____

Board Challenges

Prior to launching an endowment-building effort, it is essential that the board devise policies to guide the decision-making process. Many organizations have such policies already, but others may have to develop them. In an organization in which policies are already developed, it might be of value for the board to review and update them as appropriate for endowment.

Creating Endowment Policies

Your board may wish to review or create policies on

- Gift acceptance
- Gift reporting
- Investment
- Payout
- Endowment approval
- Acceptable endowment types
- Board use of investment principal
- Board borrowing of endowment funds

Your policies will depend on your needs and the organization's standards. For example, some organizations that plan small endowments may opt for small payouts in order to build the endowment more quickly; larger organizations with more prospects for endowment fund raising may feel more comfortable authorizing a higher payout rate. The group that works on environmental issues may create an investment policy that allows only for investment in environmentally sensitive companies.

Answer the questions posed in Worksheet 3.3 in order to create comprehensive policies to be discussed with the various committees and counsels of your endowment-building effort.

Overseeing the Endowment Fund Raising Plan

Once policies are decided upon, the board directs the endowment steering committee to develop an endowment fund raising plan for board review. The board must then oversee the establishment of a bookkeeping system and financial management system to record, report, and audit the endowment fund received by the organization, as well as select investment counsel. This counsel will invest the endowment monies and report to the board through the endowment investment committee.

WORKSHEET 3.3

Developing Policy

An organization would not be wise to accept any and all gifts, regardless of type or source. Giving careful consideration, in advance, as to what gifts are acceptable can save confusion at a later stage of your campaign and possibly prevent bad feelings among potential donors.

Gift-Acceptance Policies

1. Are there sources from which endowment funds would not be accepted?

_____

_____

_____

2. Are there uses of endowments and endowment funds that would not be acceptable?

_____

_____

_____

3. Are there donor designations that are not acceptable?

_____

_____

_____

4. Does the donor have any opportunity to change the designation?

_____

_____

_____

5. Are there kinds of gifts (such as old cars) that the organization will not accept?

_____

_____

_____

WORKSHEET 3.3 (continued)

6. At what financial levels do endowments become *named* endowments?

_____

_____

_____

Investment Policies

1. Is there an acceptable annual return on investments that the board expects?

_____

_____

2. What percentage of the annual return will the board allocate, and what percentage will remain with the fund for growth purposes?

_____

_____

3. How often will the board review the status of the endowment and its funds?

_____

_____

4. Who is authorized to make investment decisions?

_____

_____

_____

5. Are all practices consistent with the Uniform Management of Institutional Funds Act of the American Institute of Certified Accountants?

_____

_____

_____

WORKSHEET 3.3 (continued)

Endowment Funding Policies

If an endowment is not completely funded or is in the process of being funded over a period of years, the board must provide guidance to the finance officer and the development director.

1. Is the individual endowment fund income expended as the fund grows?

_____

_____

2. Is the income held until the endowment fund reaches its acceptable level?

_____

_____

3. May the donor make gifts of any kind, or must gifts be in cash or as cash equivalent?

_____

_____

Staff Challenges

Staff at all levels, from the executive director to the record keeper, are essential to the endowment team. The primary staff tasks in the partnership with volunteers are to

- Develop the preliminary working draft of the endowment-building plan
- Work closely with the endowment steering committee and volunteers
- Provide inspirational leadership for the fund raising effort

Some additional staff tasks might include

- Identifying prospective donors
- Participating in the education and cultivation of donors
- Making a contribution to endowment
- Being involved, along with volunteers, in the solicitation of prospects
- Engaging in all forms of donor recognition
- Managing the day-to-day operations of the endowment program

- Providing brochures, flyers, and case documents for use in the endowment-building effort
- Seeing that volunteers are effectively trained
- Providing moral support, coaching, and backup for volunteers
- Seeing that volunteer leaders are recognized for their efforts

Development Director's Challenges

In Chapter Two, you learned the importance of assuring the executive director that endowment fund raising can be integrated into all other fund raising without any negative impact on annual funds, major gifts, or other fund raising initiatives of your organization. Now you should be involved in the selection of the chairpersons and members of the endowment steering committee and the endowment investment committee.

Next you will work with the endowment steering committee and the executive director to devise a three-year endowment fund raising plan that includes three critical items: (1) the first proposed financial goals, (2) the development of an expense budget for endowment, and (3) the allocation of staff time and resources to endowment fund raising. A three-year plan provides adequate time for reaching goals but allows for revisiting and revising the plan before too much time elapses.

Finally, you will work closely with the chief financial officer—the staff person responsible for day-to-day financial management. The idea is to integrate all fund management under one key person, no matter how many committees, fund raising groups, or boards there are. The collaboration will ensure that financial management systems are clearly defined, understandable, defensible, and consistent with donor needs and wants, as well as to create a reporting system for endowment fund raising that ensures accurate reporting to volunteer leaders and the executive director.

Executive Director's Challenges

The executive director must commit a percentage of work time to endowment fund raising and actively engage in the cultivation, education, and solicitation of prospective endowment donors. As a part of this effort, the executive director works with the development director and finance officer to ensure that the organization's financial systems work effectively and that enough time, money, and people are in place to support the endowment initiative.

After working with the board chair to identify and recruit strong volunteer leaders for the endowment steering committee and the endowment investment committee, the executive director joins the two new committees at their first meeting. The executive director represents the prospective donors to the organization (that is, provides information about them) and represents the organization to the donors by articulating the case for endowment fund raising and providing an inspirational vision.

Finance Officer's Challenges

It is the finance officer's responsibility to (1) recommend endowment policies and investment practices, (2) maintain all documents related to the establishment of endowment funds, endowment investment practices, and endowment allocations, and (3) report regularly on the status of the endowment funds, the allocation of returns, and the use of those returns.

Some additional tasks of the finance officer might include

- Ensuring to the extent possible that returns on restricted endowments are used as directed by the donor

- Overseeing the creation and modification of endowment accounts with the auditor

- Preparing donor-stipulated reporting documents using official records of the organization

- Reviewing the investment manager's performance and working with the endowment investment committee to secure the best possible return for the institution

- Depositing all endowment-fund cash for investment

- Selling all other donated assets of tangible property

What's Next?

In the next chapter, we'll discuss the systems that must be in place to support the work of volunteers and staff.

Choosing a Fund Raising Approach

Choosing Endowment Types and Structures

Budgeting

Record Keeping

What's Next?

Building Endowment Systems

EFFICIENT AND EFFECTIVE SYSTEMS are essential to endowment fund raising success. Now that your organization has chosen the individuals who will undertake the effort, you are ready to make some critical decisions about the shape of your endowment program. Start-up will be labor-intensive, and doing it right may be frustrating at times. However, careful attention to detail will ensure that the program will be soundly based in good planning.

Choosing a Fund Raising Approach

The endowment steering committee should advise the board and staff, at the start of the endowment effort, about which fund raising approach should be taken. This is a critical decision and should be examined carefully by all involved. The choice of one strategy does not exclude the use of others; over time, the organization may choose to use several strategies. Although planned giving is the most traditional means of raising endowment, outright gifts of cash or securities can be solicited both in a campaign and in a major gift approach.

A Major Gift Approach

Most, but not all, endowment fund raising concentrates on major gifts. Because an endowment fund needs to be large enough to generate a meaningful income, large gifts must be raised. This effort focuses on the direct solicitation of one prospective donor at a time.

A major gift approach to endowment requires a strong staff commitment and staff leadership. At least some of the members of the endowment steering committee must be willing to make a major gift and able to make leadership gift calls on a few prospects if this approach is to succeed. The board and past board members might be good first prospects for this kind of approach.

A major gift approach is recommended only for nonprofits with a history of major gift fund raising and the willingness to assign staff, rather than an executive or volunteer, to the project. This kind of fund raising takes considerable management and strong personal and professional relationships. The staff person must be skilled in major gift fund raising and have some knowledge of planned giving; the person should also have solid people skills and management credentials.

A Planned Giving Approach

Planned giving is a fundamental endowment-giving option. Gifts-by-bequest, insurance, and charitable trusts are all components of a successful planned giving program. In an array of somewhat complicated gift options, the gift-by-bequest often seems the simplest to implement. Many organizations have built bequest programs as the mainstay of their endowment fund raising program.

Endowment Campaign Approach

Starting or strengthening an endowment effort with a campaign can be a productive approach. This strategy starts with the premise that endowment must be raised immediately to a high level of visibility. Then, for a short time, it should be central to the organizational fund raising effort.

An endowment fund raising campaign is organized much like a capital campaign; explicit goals and benchmarks are set, which are to be achieved within a finite time period. Structures are established that will enable the organization to raise a significant endowment over a relatively short period of time. Big dollars are in the pot, and more and more people see it and know about it.

An endowment campaign has the advantage of being high profile, mobilizing many volunteers at once, and having clearly defined goals for success. A campaign can be a catalyst for serious commitment within your organization to endowment fund raising. Its downside is pressure to obtain gifts within a time frame that may not be practical, fast burnout of volunteers, and more cash-outright gifts than long-term commitments in the form of planned gifts. (To learn more about campaigns, see *Preparing Your Capital Campaign* by Marilyn Bancel, Jossey-Bass Publishers, 2000.)

Use Worksheet 4.1 to help you choose the fund raising approach that works best for your organization.

WORKSHEET 4.1

Choosing Your Approach to Endowment

The choice of an approach to endowment fund raising depends on the strength of your current programs and the history of your fund raising.

If you answer yes to most of the following questions, a *major gift approach* may be best for you:

1. Does your organization have a history of major gift fund raising?

    ☐ Yes   ☐ No

2. Will a staff member rather than an executive or a volunteer have responsibility for the endowment fund raising?

    ☐ Yes   ☐ No

3. Does the staff member assigned to endowment fund raising have significant major gifts fund raising experience?

    ☐ Yes   ☐ No

4. Does the staff member responsible for endowment fund raising have sufficient time for one-on-one direct solicitation and major gifts management (at least fifteen hours per week)?

    ☐ Yes   ☐ No

5. Are there members of the endowment steering committee who are capable of and willing to make a major gift?

    ☐ Yes   ☐ No

6. Are your endowment steering committee members experienced in or prepared for making major gift asks?

    ☐ Yes   ☐ No

If you answer yes to most of the following questions, a *planned giving approach* may be best for you:

1. Does your organization have a planned giving program in place?

    ☐ Yes   ☐ No

2. Has your organization received at least five planned gifts in the last three years?

    ☐ Yes   ☐ No

3. Is a volunteer or the executive director responsible for endowment fund raising?

    ☐ Yes   ☐ No

4. Have members of the endowment steering committee made planned gifts to the organization, or are they considering such gifts?

    ☐ Yes   ☐ No

WORKSHEET 4.1 (continued)

5. Is your organization small and limited in resources?

   ☐ Yes   ☐ No

If you answer yes to most of the following questions, a *campaign approach* may be best for you:

1. Does your organization have experience running capital or other campaigns?

   ☐ Yes   ☐ No

2. Were those campaigns successful?

   ☐ Yes   ☐ No

3. Do you need or want to raise a significant amount for your endowment quickly?

   ☐ Yes   ☐ No

4. Do you feel that only a campaign would provide the visibility needed to get the endowment off the ground?

   ☐ Yes   ☐ No

5. Do you feel that only a campaign would provoke a serious commitment from board and staff to endowment fund raising?

   ☐ Yes   ☐ No

6. Do you have an endowment steering committee willing to act as an endowment campaign committee for the duration of the campaign?

   ☐ Yes   ☐ No

7. Are you prepared to replace your endowment steering committee with a new one if the volunteers are burned out by a campaign?

   ☐ Yes   ☐ No

Choosing Endowment Types and Structures

You learned about endowment types and structures in Chapter One. Now it is time for your endowment steering committee to explore which options can be offered to donors and what kinds of endowments the organization wants and can manage. Some or all of the options are viable either one at a time or together. These decisions will be critical to establishing good donor relationships.

The organization should determine what will be funded by the return on the invested endowment. Organizations often do not explore the wide range of available choices. The first step is to discuss with program staff (social workers, university faculty, teachers, and so on) what they see as the primary needs of the organization. This catalog of needs should not be so rigid that it does not leave room for creative donors who see a need the organization does not recognize.

Some donors may need help in deciding where to invest their gifts. It is wise for the organization to have a range of options to offer the donor; of special interest to some donors will be your day-to-day program expenses.

REAL-WORLD EXAMPLE

A donor at a private school wishes to establish a restricted scholarship endowment fund to support only left-handed students. The school, on reviewing these conditions, concludes that such terms are not in the school's best interest.

Any nonprofit may reject a gift of endowment if the terms do not appear to be in the best interest of the institution. In this case, the school went back to the donor and explained its reasons for not wanting an endowment tied to these terms. The donor was persuaded that a general unrestricted scholarship would be a more effective tool for the school. He quite willingly changed the designation.

Note, however, that a donor has a right to ask for the terms and conditions he or she wants and is not obligated to make the gift.

The choice of endowment type is often dictated by the donor. Many donors have a sense of how and when they want their money to be used, and it is best to remain flexible in order to respond to donor needs. However, depending on the size of your organization and your ability to manage funds, you may wish to choose only certain types of endowment.

True endowments are the most straightforward and easiest to account for. Discuss with your financial officer and with financial advisers on the board whether the organization has an interest in creating term and quasi-endowment funds. For most organizations just starting out, a true endowment fund is preferred.

Whether endowments are restricted or unrestricted is again often dictated by the donor. Some organizations may wish to restrict endowment funds to specific needs that are pressing and chronically underfunded, but most wish to maintain flexibility with these funds. You may decide that you will accept unrestricted funds, but beware that this may limit your fund raising abilities.

Review the descriptions of endowment types in Chapter One, then use Worksheet 4.2 to determine what kinds of endowment your organization wants, can manage, and can offer to donors, as well as how these endowments will be structured.

A large organization providing shelter for homeless families was uncomfortable about embarking on endowment fund raising for fear it would negatively affect its annual fund, which was critical to day-to-day operations. They settled on a highly focused and restricted endowment program. First, they calculated the cost of operating a unit in the shelter for a full year. Then they offered donors the opportunity to endow that annual cost with a restricted gift. Every time a unit of the shelter was endowed, funds from the operating budget were released and could be used as the organization saw fit. This endowment grew, and operating funds were sheltered. Donors could see the advantage of giving, in effect, to both endowment and operations with the same gift.

Budgeting

Now that you have decided on the infrastructure of your endowment fund raising program, you'll need to figure out how to finance it. Boards should be well educated about the financial realities of endowment fund raising. No matter what endowment types you choose, the organization will need to set aside money in the budget specifically for endowment.

Start-Up Costs

One of the special challenges of endowment fund raising is finding the seed money to underwrite the start-up. Traditionally, there have been four major sources for underwriting the up-front costs of an endowment fund raising venture:

1. *The benefactor:* Among the constituents of an organization may be an individual wise in the work of fund raising and able to provide a leadership gift to underwrite the cost of building endowment. Such a donor should be carefully cultivated and persuaded of the impact that his or her gift will have on the future of the organization.

2. *The board:* Members of the board sometimes rise to the occasion and collectively provide the financial underwriting necessary to mount an endowment effort. This board campaign should be done with the same care and careful cultivation that would be taken with any donors.

3. *Foundations:* From time to time, a foundation that believes in endowment and the power of endowment in the nonprofit world will provide a gift in advance of the endowment campaign. This gift can then be used to underwrite the cost of the campaign.

4. *Reserve funds:* Sometimes an organization is fortunate enough to have some unrestricted reserves that can be used to underwrite the cost of endowment fund raising. These funds should be returned to the reserve as the endowment grows.

WORKSHEET 4.2

Endowment Types and Structures

This worksheet will help you discover programs and projects that can be endowed. It may be wise to copy this and circulate it among staff and volunteers so they can fill in their own answers and the ideas those answers generate.

1. *Program endowment:* What specific programs does your organization have that could be endowed?

_____

_____

_____

2. *Named memorial endowment:* Are there buildings, classrooms, programs, or even staff positions that could be named?

_____

_____

_____

3. *Scholarship endowment:* Are there any educational programs that need funding? (This question is not restricted to schools; any type of patient or client education can have a scholarship attached.)

_____

_____

_____

4. *Uncompensated care endowment:* Do you have clients unable to pay for services?

_____

_____

_____

5. *Faculty or staff chair endowment:* Is there a crucial program head position that lends itself to being endowed?

_____

_____

_____

---

6. *Facilities endowment:* Does your organization spend a big piece of its budget just keeping the lights on or running the air conditioning? Would an endowment release vital funds for other programs?

   _____

   _____

   _____

7. *Buildings and grounds endowment:* Are their maintenance issues, renovation needs, or ongoing problems with buildings and grounds that drain needed funds?

   _____

   _____

   _____

8. *Staff-scholarship endowment:* Are there members of your staff who need continuous education?

   _____

   _____

   _____

   _____

9. *Technology upgrade endowment:* Is technology especially crucial to your organization?

   _____

   _____

   _____

   _____

10. *Client services endowment:* What parts of your services would be appropriate to endow?

   _____

   _____

   _____

   _____

Operating Costs

Raising endowment is usually a very low-cost venture. Endowment funds have been raised for as little as 10 percent of the total. However, it is also a front-end-loaded kind of fund raising because dollars must be expended well before income is produced.

The major costs in endowment fund raising are as follows:

- Staff salaries and benefits
- Consultant fees
- Materials development, including printing and postage
- Travel funds (in some cases)
- Events budget (cultivation activity)
- Recognition events
- Stewardship

The initial investment must include a three-year budget commitment from the board. To budget one year at a time does not acknowledge the complex relationships that evolve in endowment fund raising. Often it can take a year or more of cultivation to secure a major endowment commitment. Use Worksheet 4.3 to do a three-year budget forecast for your organization.

The budget should be developed by staff and approved by the endowment steering committee and the board finance committee. Day-to-day management is the responsibility of staff, with oversight provided by the executive director and the endowment steering committee and the board finance committee. You may also choose to bring in investment counsel. If so, take care to find counsel that has an excellent reputation and is well received by most prospective donors.

Exhibits 4.1 and 4.2 show two sample budgets you can study before using Worksheet 4.4 to create your organization's own endowment fund raising budget. Some of the items listed in the budget worksheet will be discussed in greater detail in Chapters Five and Six. The sample budgets are predicated on a three-year forecast of income and expenses. These numbers may not fit your organization precisely but are likely to represent percentages that some of these items represent in such a budget.

Be sure to examine the laws of your state regarding endowments and all the laws relevant to nonprofit organizations. You will find information either with the office of the secretary of state or the state attorney general. Also check with your auditor prior to setting up a fund to hold endowment monies. The auditor can save the organization considerable trouble in the operation, bookkeeping, and management of an endowment fund.

WORSHEET 4.3

Budget Forecast

This worksheet will help you forecast the cost of endowment fund raising over a three-year period. Complete this form as a first draft of projections for expenses and projected income. Begin a discussion with the endowment steering committee about the realities of fund raising cost.

Expense Line Item	Year 1	Year 2	Year 3
Staff salaries	_____	_____	_____
Benefits	_____	_____	_____
Consultant fees	_____	_____	_____
Printing	_____	_____	_____
Paper	_____	_____	_____
Postage	_____	_____	_____
Phone	_____	_____	_____
Travel	_____	_____	_____
Meals	_____	_____	_____
Recognition	_____	_____	_____
Total	_____	_____	_____
Percentage of Goal	_____	_____	_____

Income	Year 1	Year 2	Year 3
Case	_____	_____	_____
Pledges	_____	_____	_____
Expectancies	_____	_____	_____
Gifts-in-kind	_____	_____	_____
Cause-related marketing	_____	_____	_____
Gifts Total	_____	_____	_____
Gifts as Percentage of Goal	_____	_____	_____

EXHIBIT 4.1

Sample Budget for $100,000 Endowment

INCOME

	Individuals	$80,000	
	Foundations	$20,000	
	Corporations	$ NA	
	Community Organizations	$ NA	
	Others	$ NA	
	[Total Income]		$100,000

EXPENSES

Personnel

	Executive director	$3,000	
	Development director	$6,000	
	Campaign director	$ NA	
	Support staff	$1,500	
	Consultant(s)	$ NA	
	Other staff	$ NA	
	[Total Personnel]		$10,500

Communications

	Brochures	$500	
	Video	$ NA	
	Newsletters	$100	
	Web site	$ NA	
	[Total Communications]		$ 600

Research

	Outside firm	$ NA

Cultivation Events

	Financial planning workshops	$500	
	Luncheons	$500	
	Kick-off	$ NA	
	[Total Cultivation Events]		$ 1,000

Printing and Postage

	Letterhead	$ NA	
	Mailings	$1,000	
	Volunteer packets	$300	
	Case document	$1,000	
	Photography	$500	
	[Total Printing and Postage]		$ 2,800

Donor Stewardship

	Recognition events	$500	
	Legacy Club	$ NA	
	Tours	$ NA	
	Hospitality	$ NA	
	[Total Donor Stewardship]		$ 500
	Total Campaign Costs		$ 15,400

EXHIBIT 4.2

Sample Budget for $1 Million Endowment

INCOME

Individuals	$800,000	
Foundations	$100,000	
Corporations	$100,000	
Community Organizations	$ NA	
Others	$ NA	
Return on Investment	$ NA	
[Total Income]		$1,000,000

EXPENSES

Personnel

Executive director	$10,000	
Development director	$33,000	
Campaign director	$ NA	
Support staff	$15,000	
Consultant(s)	$5,000	
Other staff	$ NA	
[Total Personnel]		$63,000

Communications

Brochures	$5,000	
Video	$ NA	
Newsletters	$ NA	
Web site	$ NA	
[Total Communications]		$ 5,000

Research

Outside firm	$5,000	
[Total Research]		$ 5,000

Cultivation Events

Financial planning workshops	$1,200	
Luncheons	$2,500	
Kick-off	$ NA	
[Total Cultivation Events]		$ 3,700

Printing and Postage

Letterhead	$500	
Mailings	$12,000	
Volunteer packets	$500	
Case document	$2,500	
Photography	$1,000	
[Total Printing and Postage]		$16,500

Donor Stewardship

Recognition events	$2,500	
Legacy Club	$3,000	
Tours	$ NA	
Hospitality	$1,000	
[Total Donor Stewardship]		$ 6,500
Total Campaign Costs		$ 99,700

WORKSHEET 4.4

Building Your Endowment Budget

First, write down the endowment strategy that you have chosen for your organization. Is it to be a campaign or a slow and steady endowment-building process? Then write down the financial goal you have set for the campaign or first phase of the endowment effort.

Strategy: Endowment Campaign _____   Slow and Steady _____

Goal: Campaign Goal $ _____   First-Phase Goal $ _____

INCOME

	Individuals	$ _____
	Foundations	$ _____
	Corporations	$ _____
	Community organizations	$ _____
	Others	$ _____
	Return on investment	$

EXPENSES

Personnel

	Executive director	$ _____
	Development director	$ _____
	Campaign director	$ _____
	Support staff	$ _____
	Consultant(s)	$ _____
	Other staff	$ _____

Communications

	Brochure(s)	$ _____
	Video	$ _____
	Newletters	$ _____
	Web site	$ _____

Research

	Outside firm	$ _____

Cultivation Events

	Financial planning workshops	$ _____
	Luncheons	$ _____
	Kick-off	$ _____

WORKSHEET 4.4 (continued)

Printing

	Letterhead	$ _____
	Mailings	$ _____
	Volunteer packets	$ _____
	Case document	$ _____
	Photography	$ _____

Donor Stewardship

	Recognition events	$ _____
	Legacy Club	$ _____
	Tours	$ _____
	Hospitality	$ _____

Financial Management

	Audit and reporting	$ _____
	Investment counsel	$ _____
	Bank charges	$ _____

Record Keeping

Once the budget is in place and endowment fund raising has begun, efficient record keeping is vital. Record keeping is the primary responsibility of staff. Your organization needs a record-keeping system that

- Is established with the support of the auditor and the board finance committee

- Is consistent with good financial practices

- Makes it easy to report to donors

- Demonstrates that the return on individual endowments is used as directed by the donor

What's Next?

Leadership is recruited, systems are in place, and now it's time to get out and ask for the gift. In the next chapter, we address the asking process.

Identifying, Cultivating, and Soliciting Prospects

THE HEART of a successful endowment fund raising program is building relationships with prospective donors. Once you have identified prospects, your organization should develop a comprehensive marketing and communications plan, the aim of which is to cultivate these prospects. A good plan will (1) educate prospective donors about the benefits of endowment giving, (2) make the case for endowment, and (3) give your constituency an opportunity to provide feedback.

Developing a Marketing Plan

A comprehensive marketing and communications plan should be developed along with the overall endowment fund raising plan. Work with your marketing staff person and the marketing and communications committee of the board to form the plan.

A well-designed plan for endowment fund raising is almost entirely prospect- and donor-centered. The primary elements of such a plan are

Identifying target markets. Decide which groups are likely candidates for endowment fund raising.

Identifying the best communications vehicles. Consider whether mailings, meetings, newsletters, or some combination would be best.

Determining the message to be delivered to each of the constituent groups. The message is often laced with notions of what's in it for the donor, how the donor can make a difference, and what the need for endowment is in your organization.

Market testing. Before you broadcast widely, the organization and its leadership should be testing the concept of endowment with long-time donors, benefactors, and patrons. Test with the people who know and love you.

Budgeting for marketing and communications. There are substantial costs for personnel, printing, and events that should be factored into the cost of fund raising.

Articulating the Message

Before you begin printing anything, make sure you understand your organization's message and can articulate it in an interesting way. Begin by reviewing the case statement you learned to draw up earlier; select the main points; find "quotable quotes." Overall, make sure you understand your target audience.

Executing the Plan

Secret endowment fund raising does not succeed. Your organization must inform as many people as possible that you are building an endowment. In marketing and communications, it is important to recognize redundancy as a virtue. This chapter explores some unique aspects of and ideas for marketing and for communicating about endowment fund raising.

Identifying Likely Donors

Before you can cultivate and solicit prospective donors, you must identify them. In Chapter Two, you learned how to analyze your current donor base. Now it is time to look more deeply at who in the database is actually a prospective donor to your endowment and who else you might wish to approach. Some people may feel they are too young to talk about endowment. Some have few or no assets. Some want to give now for now. It is your task to find individuals who want to leave a legacy, who love your cause and wish it to continue beyond their lives, and who are ready to make a commitment to endowment.

Targeting Individuals

No one prospect falls into all of the categories shown in the following list, but people in any combination of these categories can be real and serious potential donors. Remember that today 90 percent of all endowment gifts come through bequests from individuals.

Some of these characteristics will look familiar from the donor analysis you conducted in Chapter Two. You are looking for individuals who

- Have a long history of giving to the organization
- Are age fifty or older
- Have a link to the organization

- Have given to another organization's endowment
- Have no heirs
- Have been retired for a period of time
- Currently give to your organization
- Gave in the past to your organization
- Are current board members
- Are past board members

Let's take a look at these last four categories:

Current donors: As you learned in Chapter Two, the most likely donor to your endowment is someone who is already a donor to your organization. So the first place to look is inside your organization. At least 1 percent of your current donor base consists of likely candidates for endowment giving. Examine your list, and look at the information you gathered about these donors in Chapter Two.

Past donors: Your organization should have a list of those who gave in the past but have not given recently. The failure to give annually is no sure sign that these individuals will not give to your endowment. A careful examination of the donor's history should include years of giving, total value of gifts given, size of any large gift, relationship of the donor to the organization, zip code or neighborhood, and any anecdotal information that might have accumulated; this information should enable the organization to screen the list, at least in a crude fashion. Exploring past donors' interest in endowment through mailings, focus groups, informal events, and educational meetings to describe this new initiative are other good ways to determine levels of interest.

Current board members: These individuals are already actively engaged in thinking about and building an endowment fund raising program. They have a vested interest in the success of the program. Among them are some of the best prospects for endowment gifts.

Past board members: These individuals are often untapped resources. They have a history of caring for the organization and making a commitment to it and might therefore have an interest in giving to endowment.

Targeting Corporations and Foundations

Careful research will be required to discover which foundations give to endowments for organizations such as yours. For the most part, foundations consider *themselves* to be endowments and therefore decline to give to other nonprofit endowments. However, if a corporation has a long history of giving to your organization and has a relationship that is firm and consistent, it is a prospective donor.

Corporate giving offices and corporate foundations acknowledge that they give strategically, according to what will most benefit them. You must calculate the value of giving an endowment gift to your organization *from the corporate point of view.* Not many in the nonprofit world match up well with corporate needs. If your organization cannot meet a given corporation's needs, simply move along to other sources. However, with the right focus and a set of restrictions that help the foundation meet its needs, it is possible to secure some limited endowment funds from foundations. Worksheet 5.1 will help you develop your approach to a target corporation.

Worksheets 5.2 through 5.5 will help you understand, rate, narrow down, and keep track of your prospects.

WORKSHEET 5.1

Evaluating Potential Corporate Donors

All corporations are not equally good prospects. Here are questions to consider when you're deciding which to approach.

1. What would the likely benefits be to the corporation if they chose to contribute to your organization's endowment?

   _____

   _____

   _____

2. Are there benefits that you can see and measure and that provide positive outcomes for the corporation?

   _____

   _____

   _____

3. Can you make the case for the benefits as you sit down with corporate representatives? If yes, outline the case as you understand it now.

   _____

   _____

   _____

WORKSHEET 5.2

Understanding Who Your Prospects Are

Prospecting is all about building lists. The more lists of prospects the merrier. This is an exercise that the development staff and the endowment committee of the board should do all the time. Build lists of potential prospects, explore how realistic they are, discard some, and then focus on those who seem most likely.

Answer the next questions as best you can. Over time, your answers will change as more people have more insights into the prospect base of the organization. Constantly update the list.

1. What groups or clusters of people or constituents will the prospects come from?

   _____

   _____

   _____

   _____

   _____

   _____

2. What are their characteristics?

   Average age _____

   Giving history _____

   Interest in endowment _____

   Primary connection to the organization _____

   Asset base _____

   Other _____

Rating an Endowment Prospect

Finally, you must come down to one name at a time for big gift endowment prospects. Complete this form by filling in a name to replace "John Brown." This will be the first test to tell you if you have a real prospect. You may also discover you simply do not know enough about someone and you must continue collecting information.

Is John Brown . . .

1. A person who has already made a gift to your organization?

   ☐ Yes   ☐ No

   Nature of gift: _____

2. A person whose life has been touched by your organization?

   ☐ Yes   ☐ No

   How so? _____

3. A person who has been a board member, committee member, or participant in volunteer leadership?

   ☐ Yes   ☐ No

   In what role? _____

4. A person who is very grateful for the service or programs provided by your organization?

   ☐ Yes   ☐ No

   Nature of service or program: _____

5. A person wishing to make a difference?

   ☐ Yes   ☐ No

   How so? _____

6. A person wishing to make a difference beyond his or her own life?

   ☐ Yes   ☐ No

   How so? _____

WORKSHEET 5.3 (continued)

7. A person over fifty years of age?

☐ Yes　　　☐ No

8. A person with assets of $250,000 or more?

☐ Yes　　　☐ No

Is a frequent giver _____

Is a major gift donor active in the organization _____

Has a link to the organization _____

Believes in endowment _____

Has the capacity to make a major gift _____

Is a sometime giver _____

Has made no major gifts _____

Has been active; is not now _____

Has a link to the organization _____

Has the capacity to make a major gift _____

Is uncertain about endowment _____

Has no giving history _____

Has a weak link to the organization _____

Is not active _____

Rate the Prospect　　A _____　　B _____　　C _____

Primary Contact with "John Brown"

1. Name _____

2. Steps to be taken next

Solicit _____

Cultivate _____

Educate _____

Link _____

WORSHEET 5.3 (continued)

3. How and when will the concept of endowment be introduced to this prospect?

_____

_____

4. What interests does the prospect demonstrate? _____

_____

5. Who might be the best possible solicitor? _____

6. What size endowment gift is possible?

   Range: $ _____ to $_____

7. What part of the case is most likely to appeal to this prospect?

_____

_____

_____

8. Is this a prospect for

   Cash outright gift _____

   Bequest _____

   Appreciated securities _____

   Other tangible property _____

   Charitable remainder trust _____

   Life insurance _____

9. What are the first three steps in a stewardship plan for this prospect, following the gift?

   1. _____

   2. _____

   3. _____

WORKSHEET 5.4

Ten Hot Prospects

This is a worksheet to use as you begin to identify the major gift prospects for the endowment fund raising effort. This level of detail is required so that you can distinguish the real prospects from the mythical prospects. Each component of the chart is vital to making a decision about making a fund raising solicitation.

Name: Name and address of the prospect

Link: Person or persons who know this prospect

Connection: Connection with the organization or cause

Asker: Names of the best possible askers

Rating: Dollar amount this person could give

Plan: Education, cultivation, and solicitation plan for this prospect

	Name	Link	Connection	Asker	Rating	Plan
1.						
2.						
3.						
4.						
5.						
6.						
7.						
8.						
9.						
10.						

WORKSHEET 5.5

Prospect Worksheet

Now you have determined that a person is a real prospect. Here is a simple format for working on a short list of prospects who have the potential to make big gifts to your endowment. This is the record we use as we prepare to ask for the gift. Keep it updated. It always changes.

Prospect   Name

Rating   Size of gift to be requested

Caller   Name of the person or persons to be involved in the fund raising call

Date   Date of the call as negotiated with the prospect

Prospect	Rating	Caller	Date

Building Relationships

Now that you have your prospect list, you're ready to begin building your relationships with prospective donors. There are a few basic communications approaches you may wish to initiate. Your organization may already be engaging in some or all of these strategies. In that case, you simply must ensure that information about endowment building is incorporated into existing approaches.

Communitywide Approach

This is a strategy in which the organization does a wide-ranging marketing effort to inform, educate, and engage prospective donors. Every communication vehicle is used: newsletters, brochures, direct mailings, annual fund mailings, and any other vehicle that allows the organization to deliver the following messages:

- Endowment is important to our organization.
- You can give to our endowment easily.
- You can make a difference in the future of our organization, not just its present.

These messages should be delivered often. Every opportunity to tell the story of endowment and your organization's need for it should be maximized.

Segmented and Targeted Approach

This is a strategy in which the organization looks at segments of the constituency and makes a focused approach to endowment marketing and fund raising. In this situation, the strategy is to identify and focus on those most likely to give to endowment rather than throwing as wide a net as possible.

This strategy, like the communitywide approach, can take the form of written and frequently repeated appeals and should focus on answering the key questions for the prospective donor. For a target constituency of major donors, these questions might focus not only on the need for and efficacy of an endowment but the financial and tax benefits to the donor as well.

One-on-One Approach

This strategy requires the identification of individual prospective donors. The creation of a plan to cultivate and educate those donors requires that very specific marketing materials be designed for each individual and that a tailored ask be designed to elicit a commitment to endowment. In these cases, research is crucial. For example, if research reveals that a past board member has no heirs, owns a home that is highly valuable, and made a planned gift to another organization, you might design an ask based on the prospect's knowledge of planned giving, need to dispose of the house, and past involvement with your organization.

Choosing Cultivation Methods

For the prospective donor to know the answer to the question, "What's in it for me?" you must communicate regularly and frequently. Your cultivation strategies will evolve as you identify potential prospects and receive feedback on your efforts. Although many vehicles can be used, those listed here are specifically geared toward endowment fund raising. The choice of vehicles often depends on what market you think is most likely to respond to your need, your resources, and your goals and time line.

Mailings and Postscripts

Direct mail can include a response instrument. Although these mailings get a very low percentage of responses (from .5 to 1.0 percent), those who do respond are seriously interested and are willing to expose their interest to the organization. Thus direct mail gives the organization the opportunity to send those who respond more materials and even to call on them.

At this point, you must ask yourself whether your direct mail piece creates an exchange that is beneficial to the prospective donor. For example, these mailings should provide some useful information to the prospect, possibly about financial planning or about writing a will.

Some organizations include a postscript on all solicitation materials, response cards, and so on, as a way of finding out whether the receiver is interested in talking about or receiving information about naming the organization in his or her will, making a planned gift, or making a gift to endowment. This postscript serves as a constant reminder that this kind of giving is important to the organization; those who respond are identified as bona fide prospects.

Financial Planning Meetings

More often associated with planned giving than endowment fund raising, this traditional offering to possible donors has the potential to clarify individuals' interest in your endowment. The organization secures the volunteer support of a good financial planner and asks that person to offer a comprehensive financial planning workshop (usually two hours or less) as a service to the constituency of the organization.

Of course, the planning program will include a clear reference to charitable giving, charitable gift instruments, and the potential for all donors to include a charitable gift in their financial plan. Because of the potential conflict of interest (the planner is not simply providing free education but may be seeking clients as well), it would be wise if the financial planner were not a member of your board; the organization should also be clear with participants about the possibility that the presenter wishes to recruit them as clients.

Focus Groups

Nonprofit organizations have used a focus group model to open the discussion of endowment with key prospects in a very productive way. Small groups of constituents with some history of support for the organization are invited to a meeting with key organizational leaders to talk about an endowment initiative for the organization.

They are asked their opinions about the concept, the organization's potential, and other endowment fund raising efforts in the community. Their views and opinions are considered in structuring the endowment program. In addition, of course, the organization has the opportunity to plant the seeds of endowment giving in the minds of these prospects. Focus groups are part of a very effective education and cultivation process.

One-on-One Calls

Individuals, generally from the endowment steering committee who have made the initial gifts to your endowment, are asked to take a friend to lunch or breakfast and simply tell them about the endowment effort and carefully report their response to the idea. This might include board members, past board members, and other friends of the organization.

Individuals who agree to conduct such meetings will need training, scripts, and back-up materials that can be left with the prospect. Staff should provide this support.

Donor Recognition as Incentive

Donor recognition can be used as a stimulus to provoke others to think about giving to your endowment. Take every opportunity to acknowledge and recognize donors to your endowment. Public celebration of gifts is an excellent way to plant the seeds of endowment giving. Large constituencies are often difficult to reach, even with direct mail. Newsletters, special bulletins, ceremonies, celebrations, and other activities can be used as vehicles for telling the story. By showcasing these gifts, you not only model what someone might consider doing but also bring the endowment effort alive with real people making real gifts that make a real difference.

Challenge Gifts

Corporations, foundations, and individuals might be solicited for challenge gifts. A challenge gift, unlike a matching gift, requires the organization to raise the money before any of the challenge money is received. So even though it might match the donor one-for-one, the money does not come until the individual gift is committed. These gifts provide an incentive for donors to give with an understanding that their gift will be matched or multiplied in some way. Some corporations and foundations like to make challenge grants and will accept such a proposition in the formal proposal format.

Matching Gifts

In this situation, a corporation, foundation, or individual decides to provide a gift on a matching basis. For example, your organization raises $100,000, and the matcher gives you $50,000. This is not premised on individual donors giving but rather on the combination of all fund raising efforts. Like challenge gifts, this provides an incentive for classes of donors and individual donors.

Unique Characteristics of the Endowment Solicitation

The conversation with the prospect about endowment involves concepts, ideals, and information that are not discussed during other types of fund raising: legacy, perpetuity, memorializing, and after-life giving. Endowment conversations are powerful because the content includes recognition of death, a commitment of estate assets, and an impact of the gift on family. Because endowment is such a powerful concept, care must be taken to respect prospective donors' privacy, personal interest, and values.

Key Principles of Solicitation

These concepts and ideas are solidly grounded in past practice and experience. They work!

- Seek large gifts before small gifts.
- Solicit inside prospects before outside prospects. Those closest to the organization are the most likely prospects.
- Remember that everybody has an estate. The vast majority of people could find a way to leave you in their will if they had a will and if they chose to do so.
- Remember that everything takes longer than you think it will.

Endowment fund raising involves such important matters that, by its very complex nature, it simply takes a long time. Patience is therefore an essential component of every endowment-building effort.

Sequence of Solicitation

Here are the people you should solicit and the order in which you should solicit them:

1. The current governing board and past board members
2. Staff (in a low-key effort that offers the opportunity for them to consider giving)
3. Corporations and foundations
4. Individuals
5. The constituency and friends

Provide the donor with a trustworthy individual with whom to negotiate this important gift.

Congratulations! You've successfully solicited your first endowment gift. Exhibit 5.1 provides an example of an official agreement form for your organization and the donor to sign. Exhibit 5.2 is a sample of a document confirming that an endowment account may now be set up.

EXHIBIT 5.1

Sample Endowment Agreement

The _____ Endowment Fund at the Friends Home for Boys

1. This agreement, dated _____ between _____ and the Friends Home for Boys, establishes the _____ Endowment Fund.

   This endowment account consists of monies irrevocably given and to be given to the Friends Home for Boys by _____ .

   This endowment account is established with an initial gift of $ _____ , given on _____ .

2. The income from this endowment will be used to provide _____ for _____ . (Here you will wish to add specifics regarding the use of the gift, including criteria for choosing recipient individuals or projects.)

   The _____ will have administering control over income from this endowment.

   If it is determined by the board that any portion of earned income is not spent for the designated purpose within a reasonable time frame after a fiscal year, it will be returned to principal.

3. The Friends Home for Boys agrees to

   a. Hold and preserve the fund as a permanent endowment fund. The board fully intends to direct income for the endowment for the purpose outlined above. However, if the purpose for which the endowment income is spent should cease to exist, the board reserves the right to direct the income of the endowment to a purpose as close as possible to the donor's original intent.

   b. Invest and manage the fund consistent with guidelines outlined by the board; endowment funds will be pooled for investment purposes.

   c. Not expend any of the principal of the fund without approval by the board.

This agreement is made on _____ by _____ .

Donor _____

Friends Home for Boys President _____

EXHIBIT 5.2
Sample Endowment Proposal Request

To: Endowment Committee of the Board

From: _____

Re: Endowment Proposal Request

The attached endowment agreement meets the financial and development acceptance guidelines of the Friends Home for Boys.

An endowment account may be established to receive gifts designated for the _____ Endowment Fund.

Reviewed by:

Chair, Endowment Committee _____

CFO _____

Executive Director _____

Chair, Finance Committee _____

What's Next?

Keeping donors is equally as important as getting donors. In the next chapter, we outline stewardship strategies for our endowment programs.

CHAPTER 6

Stewardship

MANY ENDOWMENT DONORS want and deserve a lifetime relationship with your organization. They have made a significant commitment of personal resources affecting their estate. The services your organization offers the donor on an ongoing basis will help you establish the basis for good donor relations: trust and confidence, shared values, and personal connections.

DEFINITION

Stewardship: Taking care of the relationship with the donor after the gift

---

Financial Reporting

Donors expect that your organization will report regularly on the status of their gift, including the impact their gift is having and the financial status of the fund they created. This accountability builds confidence in the organization and reconfirms that the gift makes a difference. The responsibility of reporting to donors falls squarely on the shoulders of staff and volunteer leaders. Some reporting efforts can be tied to formal institutional reporting documents such as monthly financial statements.

Providing Exposure to Programs

Donors who support specific programs or activities often want to know more about them. Some would especially enjoy a chance to be exposed to the programs or projects that are being funded. It is not unusual, for example, for a scholarship endowment donor to want to meet the recipient of the scholarship and to follow his or her success at school.

Encouraging Active Roles

Some individuals who have made a commitment to endowment want a more active role in the organization. If they have the expertise and energy the board requires, they might even be candidates for membership on the board. Some want a link to the board without the responsibility of being on it. As nonboard members, they might serve on a standing committee or be assigned to a task group charged with specific responsibilities in policy development.

Communicating Regularly and Being Inclusive

Regular communication is vital to stewardship. The following types of mailings are particularly well suited to the task:

The newsletter: If your organization publishes a newsletter, it would be appropriate to add articles, a supplementary page, donor recognition pieces, or financial reports. This newsletter can often be the device used to reinforce the importance of endowment gifts to the organization and to celebrate them. Frequent mention of endowment in the newsletter is another vital factor in keeping prospects thinking about endowment giving.

You might wish to create a newsletter that focuses on your endowment program or campaign. Send it periodically to key donors to outline the progress of your effort, highlight a few key gifts, restate the case and need, and honor donors.

Annual reports: If your organization does a formal annual report to constituents, it would be appropriate to use that document to report the success of the campaign both financially and in other ways.

Private letter: This is a letter from the executive director to major donors, prospective major donors, and others of influence in the organization. A private letter provides individuals with inside information that gives them a sense of ownership of the endowment effort.

Final campaign report: At the conclusion of an endowment campaign, there should be a published campaign report outlining the success of the effort, honoring donors, recognizing campaign leaders, and restating the impact of the new endowment on the organization.

Personal phone call: Board members and other leaders should be assigned a single stewardship call a month and, from time to time, a stewardship visit with a donor.

Donor clubs: Donor clubs can be extremely successful as part of an endowment effort. Many organizations create groups called heritage clubs or something similar as a way to attract endowment donors and as a vehicle for endowment stewardship. In many instances, these groups serve to encourage donors to continue to add to their endowments, to make outright gifts to meet special needs, and to stay linked to the cause. Donors also like the affiliation with other donors who have accomplished a similar goal. People want to know who else is giving to endowment and, in some cases, to have an opportunity to meet with and work with them.

A heritage club is composed of a few major gift donors to endowment. Donors might make a commitment of at least $50,000 in cash by bequest or other planned gift instrument. The subsequent strategy is to begin one gift at a time to build the membership of this donor club. The initial goal may be to have as many as fifty such donors over a three-year period. Goals should be set to have a certain number of members by a fixed time. The result often is few gifts and a great deal of money in endowment.

Inclusion on the endowment committee of the board: The recruitment of volunteer leaders should always include a review of donor lists. Often people who make a financial commitment are also willing to (and even want to) volunteer and invest their time.

Engagement in fund distribution from restricted endowments: Family members might meet annually to distribute the return on a family endowment that was established to honor a deceased family member. This provides the opportunity for the family to know more about the good work being done and to be certain the funds are going where they want them to go.

Your Ongoing Commitment

Your ongoing commitment to stewardship is both labor-intensive and costly. Yet the ultimate benefits of taking care of your donors far outweigh any costs associated with the effort. This is an institutional, generational responsibility. Staff and volunteers may leave, but the stewardship responsibility remains. Keep the fire burning brightly in the hearts of your donors. That's what makes great philanthropists.

A Checklist for Your Complete Endowment-Building Process

GOOD ENDOWMENT FUND RAISING starts with good planning and a careful, disciplined approached. This checklist will help you stay in touch with the progress you are making. Your organization may not proceed in exactly this order, and some of these steps need to be done on an ongoing basis, but this checklist represents an approach that has been successful for many organizations. Check and date each box as the action proceeds.

Date	Action
_____	Board creates an endowment advisory committee
_____	Advisory committee evaluates the commitment of staff and resources
_____	Staff develops a case for endowment
_____	Staff builds support for endowment within the organization
_____	Advisory committee reports to the board on its determinations or study results
_____	Board authorizes a feasibility study (if one is recommended)
_____	Board reviews the report
_____	Endowment advisory committee recruits a permanent endowment committee and other campaign committees, including an endowment investment committee

_____   Staff develops a basic endowment fund raising plan

_____   Staff and board identify prospects

_____   Staff develops a marketing and communications plan

_____   Board endorses the plan and basic policies

_____   Staff and board cultivate prospects

_____   Staff, volunteers, and board members solicit prospects

_____   Donors make endowment agreements with the organization

_____   Organization follows up with ongoing stewardship of the gift

Recommended Resources

Armstrong, S. "Here's to Bigger Endowments in the Big Sky State." *Foundation News & Commentary*, Sept.-Oct. 1998, *39*, 21–23.

Barnes, S., and Cornwell, J. L. "Building Your Endowment with Life Insurance." *Nonprofit World*, Mar.-Apr. 1990, *8*, 15–18.

Beaird, S. *Building an Endowment.* Washington, D.C.: National Catholic Educational Association, May 1999.

Billitteri, T. J. "Saving for the Future." *Chronicle of Philanthropy*, Dec. 3, 1998, 27–30.

Billitteri, T. J. "Endowment Assets Nationwide Climb to Nearly $600 Billion, New Study Finds." *Chronicle of Philanthropy*, June 15, 2000, *12*, 46.

Bryce, H. J. "Starting an Endowment: The Basics." *NonProfit Times*, Apr. 1990, *4*, 31, 36.

"Community Leaders in Eight Rural Iowa Counties Set Up Endowment Funds." *501(c)(3) Monthly Letter*, Feb. 1998, *18*, 9.

Desruisseaux, P. "Universities Venture into Venture Capitalism." *Chronicle of Higher Education*, May 26, 2000, *46*, A44–45.

Dunlop, D. R. "Get the Facts on Flexible Endowments." *Currents*, Mar. 1998, *14*, 29–34.

Ethics and the Nation's Voluntary and Philanthropic Community. INDEPENDENT SECTOR, 1991.

Fry, R. P., Jr. *Nonprofit Investment Policies: Practical Steps for Growing Charitable Funds.* New York: Wiley, 1998.

Guthrie, K. M. *The New York Historical Society: Lessons from One Nonprofit's Long Struggle for Survival.* San Francisco: Jossey-Bass, 1996.

Hall, P. D. "Endowment vs. Empowerment." *Grantsmanship Center Magazine*, Winter 1998, *34*, 7–8.

Hartsook, R. F. "Endowment Fundraising Made Easy." *Fund Raising Management,* June 1997, *28,* 30–31.

Leggett, K. E. "Your Annual, Capital, and Endowment Campaigns." *FRI Monthly Portfolio,* July 1998, *37,* 1–2.

Marshall, J. E., III. "Building Nonprofit Endowments." *Foundation News & Commentary,* Jan.-Feb. 1998, *39,* 15–17.

McLelland, R. J. "Essentials of Endowment Stewardship." *Currents,* Sept. 1997, *23,* 28–33.

Moerschbaecher, L. S. *Building an Endowment Right from the Start.* Chicago: Precept Press, 2001.

Newman, B. L., and Luckes, D. R. "Community Foundations: A Potential Endowment-Building Partner." In J. R. Alford (ed.), *Building and Managing an Asset Base.* New Directions for Philanthropic Fundraising, no. 14. San Francisco: Jossey-Bass, 1997.

Newman, B. L., and Luckes, D. R. "A Perfect Match." *Advancing Philanthropy,* Winter 1997–1998, *5,* 32–36.

Newman, R. H. "Eleven Must Do's for a Successful Capital or Endowment Fund Campaign." *Fund Raising Management,* Feb. 2000, *30,* 30–31.

Olson, R. L. *The Independent Fiduciary: Investing for Pension Funds and Endowment Funds.* New York: Wiley, 1999.

Poderis, T. "Endowment Funds Go On Forever: An Endowment Campaign Should Not." *Taft Monthly Portfolio,* Dec. 1999, *38,* 1–2.

Prenatt, S. L. "The Endowment Goose and Its Golden Egg." *Journal of Accountancy,* 1995, *180*(3).

Public Management Institute. *How to Build a Big Endowment.* San Francisco: Datarex Corporation, 1985.

Recer, J. D. *Terms of Endowment: How Board Members Can Acquire the Big Gift.* Stevensville, Md.: Eastern Shore Publishing, 1998.

Reiss, A. H. "States Establish Endowment Funds to Ensure Long-Term Arts Support." *Fund Raising Management,* Feb. 1999, *29,* 20–21, 41.

Riley, T. "Them As Has, Gets: The Problem of the Profitable Nonprofit." *Philanthropy,* May-June 2000, *14,* 32–34.

Schmeling, D. G. "Stewardship of Endowment." *Fund Raising Management,* Feb. 1996, *26,* 17–19.

Steuerle, C. E. *Will Donor-Advised Funds Revolutionize Philanthropy?* Washington, D.C.: Urban Institute, 1999.

Wheat, C. "Campaign for Dignity Makes History." *Fund Raising Management,* July 1998, *29,* 23–25.